# The Naked Chef Takes Off

Jamie Oliver
The Naked Chef Takes Off

HYPERION New York

to my missus . . .

sorry,

the lovely Jules x

*Also by Jamie Oliver*
The Naked Chef

Published by arrangement with MICHAEL JOSEPH / the Penguin Group

Typeset in 10/15 Helvetica Neue Light
Typeset by Rowland Phototypesetting Limited, Bury St. Edmonds, Suffolk
Printed in Great Britain by Butler & Tanner, Frome, Somerset

Library of Congress Cataloging-in-Publication Data.

Oliver, Jamie
        The naked chef takes off / Jamie Oliver.—1st ed.
            p.  cm.
        Includes index.
        ISBN 0–7868–6755–8
        1. Cookery.

    TX714 .046 2001
    641.5—dc21

                                                    2001024098

FIRST EDITION

10  9  8  7  6  5  4  3  2  1

# contents

**introduction**

Blimey, what a year! If I had been told a year and a half ago that I would be sitting here now writing my second book as a follow-up to *The Naked Chef* I would never have believed it. Having the chance to write the first was amazing, but to be allowed another crack of the whip is just superb. And am I ready for it? Yes, surrounded by the pukka people at Hyperion, good friends and family, you better believe it. I'm really hyped about it!

As you can imagine, being the youngest chef on the block, having a bestselling book as well as a cracking television series, not to mention being a bit scruffy and coming from Essex, I have come in for quite a bit of stick from folk. I don't mind. In fact, I quite enjoy it. It makes me laugh. This book isn't about cheffy food, it's for normal people who want shortcuts and tips; people who want to make simple day-to-day meals different and absolutely fantastic or something a little bit more fruity and indulgent. At the end of the day, it's for everyone who is interested in cooking tasty, gutsy, simple, commonsense food and having a right good laugh at the same time. That's what food's all about. It's not just about eating. To me it's about passing the potatoes around the table, ripping up some bread, licking my fingers, getting tipsy and enjoying the company of good friends or family. Pass us the mustard, Dad.

The response to *The Naked Chef* from the media and
thought that I would have been asked to cook at No. 10 for
meeting? What a great buzz that was. Or hearing Zoë Bal
tuna for dinner? Can't get better than that. Or having Mrs.
I'm washing my hair. And some of the letters I received
saying they've cooked from the book for the in-laws in dodgy

There was one occasion when I thought I would have to
of the road shouted out, "Oi, you, Naked! Come 'ere. I want
me, I waited for him to walk over, only for him to say in an
kitchen three nights a week cos my missus says if that
weeks if I'd a seen ya, I'd a knocked your 'ead off." Then his
it. I think I'm a good chef. So thanks, mate, respect." And I
bill." And then there were the old ladies in Sheffield – right
said, "OK, love, sign us this book here. Make sure there's
and we love your lingo, don't we, Gwenda?" "Yes, yes, we do,
you with your clothes on. Can't you get your kit off?" Now I
like a beet. I wanted to say something smart back but

I've spoken to loads of strangers while shopping in the
me constructive feedback. This has probably taught me the
massively influenced my approach to this book. Yeah, I still
Naked Chef: using the *bare* essentials of your larder and
But I'm also keen to make use of new ingredients which are
and legumes to fresh herbs and oils from different regions
and quality will definitely improve. P.S. Check out the index

he public has been absolutely fantastic. Who would have
Tony Blair and the Italian prime minister at their summit
on Radio 1 say that she'd cooked Fatboy Slim my seared
Merton offer me her baked pasta recipe? Not today, love,
were fantastic. It's amazing getting a letter from someone
situations and scored massive brownie points. God bless ya.
eg it, because some bloomin' great geezer over the other side
a word." Holding on to my vitals, with my life flashing before
aggressive voice, "Thanks to you, mate, I'm in the bleedin'
blond young boy can do it, so can you. For the first couple of
voice softened and he said, "I really enjoy it now I've got into
said, "Thanks, mate. All the best. I'll send you the laundry
tigers they were. While constantly patting my bottom they
kisses on it. Now, we love your program, we love your book
Maureen. Pukka, wicked it is. But we're a bit surprised to see
don't get embarrassed easily, but these OAPs had me blushing
every time I opened my mouth I sounded like Scooby-Doo.
supermarkets and walking down the street who have given
most about what real people at home really want and it has
believe in the two things that resulted in my name of the
*stripping* down restaurant methods to the reality of home.
now being stocked in your average supermarket, from fruits
of the world. If we all support these ingredients, then variety
where you'll find the V sign pointing out the vegetarian recipes.

# make life easy

Before you start cooking, I can't stress enough how much every kitchen should be stocked with the basics. Do this once and get it done properly instead of buying bits and pieces. Buy the ingredients listed below, which I promise won't cost you the earth and will keep you in good stead for the coming year.

**cupboard stuff**

**spices**

**fresh stuff**

cont...
rice : basmati, risotto (Arborio or Carnaroli)
capers : salted
olives : black and green
soy sauce
fish sauce
oyster sauce
tinned whole peeled plum tomatoes
sun-dried tomatoes (dried or in oil)
dried mushrooms (porcini)
chocolate : good quality cooking (70% cocoa solids)
cocoa powder (70% chocolate)
spices

Black peppercorns
Dried chillies
Nutmeg
Cloves
Coriander seeds
Fennel seeds
Cumin seeds
Caraway seeds
Fenugreek seeds

a bowl of lemons
a couple of limes
garlic
ginger
onions and s
chillies
potatoes
herbs

## cupboard stuff

- Oils: extra-virgin olive, olive, sunflower
- Vinegars: red wine, white wine, balsamic, rice wine
- Mustards: Dijon, wholegrain, English
- Salt: sea, table, cooking
- Sugar: brown, white, confectioners', superfine
- Flour: all-purpose, bread, cake, self-rising, strong pasta (fine strong) Tipo "00"
- Baking powder, baking soda, cornstarch
- Couscous
- Dried pasta: spaghetti, linguine, tagliatelle, penne, farfalle
- Legumes (dried or canned): cranberry beans, cannellini, black-eyed peas, lima beans, yellow split peas, lentils, chickpeas
- Rice: long-grain, basmati, arborio, carnaroli
- Anchovies in olive oil or salt
- Capers: salted (small ones are best)
- Olives: black, green
- Soy sauce, fish sauce, oyster sauce
- Canned whole peeled plum tomatoes, sun-dried tomatoes (dried or in oil)
- Dried mushrooms: porcini
- Chocolate, semisweet or bittersweet: good-quality 70% cocoa solids
- Unsweetened cocoa powder

## fresh stuff

Obviously fresh stuff is perishable but there are still some basic things that you will always use. I try to have these ingredients available all the time (see opposite list).

## spices

Spices are a must (see opposite). They're nonperishable and they're generally as cheap as chips. The fact that an essential spice and flavoring from a certain part of the world can be kept in your kitchen just waiting to be used is fantastic. By lightly roasting and/or pounding, the spices come alive in smell and flavor. There are classic combinations involved in curries, stews and seasonings, but just a single spice with salt and pepper and a little olive oil can turn an ordinary piece of fish or meat into a more classy, subtle and interesting meal. Generally, I prefer to go to small ethnic shops for my spices, as they tend to be better produced, sourced and stored. And they're a hell of a lot cheaper than your supermarkets or delis.

# potty about herbs

I'm mad about herbs—so much so that I actually have dreams about seeing big patches of them and feeling the utmost pleasure at having them right there at my culinary disposal (how weird). They're an absolute must for any kitchen, whether at home or in a restaurant. I split fresh herbs up into two sections: *hardy* herbs and *delicate* herbs. Here's my advice for getting them at their best and cheapest.

## fresh herbs

### hardy herbs

I'm not a gardener, and I certainly haven't got green fingers, but having grown a selection of rosemary, bay, thymes, sages, marjoram, oregano and mint in window-boxes and pots over the last six years, I reckon I've had enough experience to tell you that it's so cheap and dead easy to do. It doesn't matter where you live, or how much space you've got—I've only ever had a garden once (the rest of the time it's been windowboxes for me) and even then I found that potted herbs suited me best. Just spending $25 or so on a selection of herbs will give you an exciting range of flavors and you'll have them right there at your disposal—just with a snip of your scissors. So here's how to pot them, bearing in mind that you don't have to pot from seeds:

- *From seed*

Simply scatter your chosen seeds over some good organic soil in a seed tray. Place them somewhere warm and sunny, and keep them watered. When they have sprouted to about 1 inch high, transfer the seedlings into small pots.

- *Small pot*

Obviously the ideal place to grow your seedlings to the size of the classic market- or store-bought herb is a greenhouse, but a south-facing windowsill will serve just as well. Good soil, good drainage and a small, but consistent, amount of water every other day will ensure a hardy, tasty baby herb, ready to be planted outside.

- *Transplanting*

You can buy herbs ready for planting in the garden or you can use your own baby herbs grown from seed (see page 16). Carefully remove the herb plant from its pot and transplant it into your garden, windowbox, hanging baskets or large terra-cotta pots. Make sure you scatter a layer of stones on the bottom of the pot, then some good organic soil, before putting the plant on top. This will ensure good drainage. The larger the amount of soil around the herb, the bigger the plant will grow, so bear this in mind.

When transplanting herbs I tend to use the bigger, more substantial ones like rosemary, bay and sage to shape a bed or pot. The gaps can be filled in with thymes, marjoram and oregano—all are ideal. Mint spreads itself around like mad, and might be better in a pot on its own.

If you think your herbs need moving to a larger pot or space in your garden at any time, then feel free to do this.

- *Picking and pests*

Try to pick the new shoots, to encourage the plant into more growth and fullness. Herbs such as oregano and mint tend to die back in cold weather but they grow back with a vengeance in the warmer half of the year. Grow chamomile and yarrow near your herbs to keep them healthy, and deter slugs with crushed glass or Vaseline-smeared pot rims. To get rid of aphids, add a small amount of detergent to some water in a watering can and use this at the first sign of trouble (make sure you wash your herbs thoroughly before using them).

*delicate herbs*

Quite frankly, I've never had success with growing delicate herbs like parsley, basil, cilantro and tarragon. You need a good amount of nutritious soil in a sheltered, light part of the garden, which I've never had (aah), and they will only last for the summer. Lots of my friends have had success using large pots inside the kitchen on a bright windowsill, but I'm far too impatient so I just buy nice big bunches from the market.

## dried herbs

Two scenarios here:

1.  The herbs are doing so well they've gone mad and are nicking too much space in the garden or pot, so I have to be brutal and cut back the guilty ones to let the others breathe. I then simply bunch up the bits I've cut back, tie them together and hang them up to dry in a warm place (near a boiler, above an oven or just by some hot pipes). They will take about a week to dry out completely.

2.  I've bought too many herbs from the market or supermarket and I've only used half. I'm not going to be cooking for the next day or two, so I lay them out on a tray and put them in a warm place. Leave them out near the washing machine or something that generates a little bit of heat. Delicate herbs take anything from a day to a week to dry completely and they have so much more flavor and character than your dried sawdusty herbs in packets. Once dried they can be stored in airtight containers for months.

morning glory

ben

me

I grew up with a mother who cooked us breakfast every single morning, whether it was an unbeatable bacon sarnie, the full monty or her homemade jam and thick-cut bread. She was a star. Now looking back I can really appreciate how well looked after I was, especially when I compare myself to other friends who just got given a bowl of shredded wheat and some low-fat milk. "Breakfast—it's the most important meal of the day," is what she used to say. My mother was never a worrier but I think she felt a sense of relief if she sent me out the door with a good breakfast inside me because she knew that whatever else happened, I wouldn't starve for the day. She also used to say that your brain needs feeding and that it is at its most effective from seven until eleven in the morning. I'm sure she's right but it didn't do me any good. I still failed miserably at everything apart from art and geology at school, and career-wise I couldn't really see myself as an artistic geologist—all that paint and mud, ooh no.

I think breakfast is one of the most outrageously underrated luxuries in the whole world. Even London as it stands, with its wide variety of restaurants, still offers very little in the way of breakfast. Instead of meetings over lunch or dinner, why not meetings over breakfast? Instead of greasy plastic chairs, why not airy, spacious, fresh and classy diners that serve breakfast from six in the morning until midday? Blooming fantastic; I'd be there. Instead of ingredients bought from the nearest convenience store, with their classic vacuum-packed bacon and battery eggs, why not a great variety of dry-cured, thick-cut organic bacon and beautiful, golden, free-range eggs from our farmers? After all, there are some places that are still doing it properly — it's just a matter of finding them. Fresh juices, self-composed mueslis and homemade breads. I should open up a breakfast diner now before anyone else does—I'd clean up!

The idea of this chapter is not necessarily to make you or your family start eating breakfast every morning. But quite frankly, after a week's work, when the old Saturday and Sunday mornings come along, you don't always have the imagination or the foresight to knock up a quick bit of interesting brekkie for yourself, your family or your partner. If you're after some brownie points and you're a bloke, I would highly suggest breakfast in bed for the missus to give you a lucky day, and if you're like my missus, sorry, the lovely Jules, you should attempt a little bit of brekkie for your fella before asking him for a bit of cash for that dress that you've seen in Top Shop. But seriously, before Women's Lib get on the phone, I have so many

fantastic memories of breakfast with buddies and I think you'll find some interesting and different things to add to your brekkie repertoire in this chapter. If you know where Pop-Tarts orig-inated from, then let me know and I'll be over to have some serious words . . . I think it must be in Essex somewhere.

# bacon sarnie my stylie

Simple, you may think, but a good bacon sarnie has challenged many chefs, hotels and greasy spoons in England and elsewhere for years and years. There is a key to this recipe and in my view this is the way to do it.

You need the best dry-cured bacon you can get hold of. This generally means you won't get the shrinkage and watery residue from cooking like you do with most bacon these days. Shame, as we British folk used to be extremely good at rearing and curing good bacon. Second, I would suggest that you try to get hold of thicker-cut bacon, not the wafer-thin stuff that became fashionable a few years ago—you need something you can really get your teeth into. Third, I buy a small, fresh sandwich loaf (gotta be white unless you need your roughage), which should be around 10 inches long. I then cunningly and politely ask the baker to slice it lengthwise, instead of across as normal. I do this all the time and it's great. It's purely a visual thing but it seems to make it taste better to me—I don't know why. I've always been a strange boy.

So, you've got your bacon and your bread. You could quite easily go ahead and cook your bacon and toast your bread under the grill. Lovely. But if you fancy yourself as a bit of a tiger then acquire a ridged skillet, which I get as hot as possible (about 4 minutes on the highest heat) and then begin to grill about 4 slices of bacon (per person if you're greedy like me). After about 1 minute you can turn the bacon over and it will be golden with those funky charred marks across that I also think benefit the flavor slightly. Cook the other side for 1 more minute. At this point I shuffle all the bacon up one end of the pan to carry on cooking a little longer while I toast my 2 long pieces of bread in the pan. What I love about this way of doing it is that the bread soaks up just a little (not a lot) of the fat that has cooked out of the bacon which makes it even more tasty. When it has toasted on both sides you could butter your toast—I don't bother—and lay your bacon across each slice. Squeeze the 2 slices of bread together. Now it's ready to be eaten, preferably with HP or brown sauce. In the past I have also added halved tomatoes and mushrooms to the pan, which do go down very well in the sarnie too.

## midnight pan-cooked breakfast

Me and this dish go back a long way. To the pre-shaving days of being an underage drinker down at the Wagon and Horses pub in Saffron Walden [in England] with a fake ID and all my village mates. Only once in a while of course. But seriously, without trying to sound like a lagered-up geezer, I think everyone's experienced the need for food around midnight, whether the binge was small or large, otherwise why would all-night kebab shops be so popular? Anyway, I always used to have three or four friends back to my house for munchies or to stay the night, and this dish was devised so we didn't have too much trouble making it or too much washing up to do. In actual fact, I only had to wipe the nonstick pan clean. It also makes its way from the pan to the plate quite quickly, as patience isn't a virtue at that time of night with my mates!

First of all, get the biggest nonstick pan available, and preheat it on a high heat while you gather your ingredients. Obviously you wouldn't be organized at this point so it's a matter of using what you've got, but ideally I like to have mushrooms, bacon, tomatoes, sausages and eggs. By the time you have got these together the pan will be hot, so slice your sausages in half lengthwise and pat them out flat so they cook quickly. Place into the pan at one side. On the other side, put a tiny glug of oil and place a pile of mushrooms over it that you can rip up or leave whole. Shake the pan about a bit to coat the mushrooms and season with some salt and pepper. Push to one side and then lay some slices of bacon and halved tomatoes in the pan. Cook for a couple more minutes until the bacon is crisp and golden. Shake the pan and turn the bacon over. Now is the time to put a slice of toast in the toaster.

At this stage you should respect the rustic and authentic look and shuffle everything about so that it's all mixed together and add 2 or 3 eggs at different sides of the pan. The whites of the eggs will dribble in and around the sausages, bacon, tomatoes and mushrooms. Turn the heat down a little and continue to cook for another minute before placing the pan under the broiler and finishing the eggs to your liking. Using a nonstick pan I've always found the removal of this dish to the plate extremely easy—it will resemble a Frisbee and will slide onto your plate with no trouble at all. Doesn't that sound appetizing? But honestly, it really is a gem.

## figs, honey and ricotta

I first had this in Florence for brekkie and my initial reaction, as the unworldly person that I am, was why am I having cheese for breakfast? But this combination of perfect figs and honey is amazing, different and damn tasty.

Before you say you don't like figs . . . that's what I used to say, remembering chewing on tough, tasteless old figs that you would have to peel the skin off. But I have been converted because the shops and supermarkets are starting to get hold of really good fresh figs, both green and purple. Slightly firm on the outside, soft and sometimes sticky in the middle, with an amazing sweet taste—unlike anything else.

There's no point in me giving you amounts for this recipe as, quite frankly, you can have as much or as little as you like. Myself, I normally go along the one fig per person vibe. Score a crisscross across the top of the fig to about halfway down, then gently squeeze the base of the fig. It will pucker up and look extremely funky, and helps us by exposing a little of the inside which we can dribble honey in. Place the fig beside a slice of fresh ricotta from the deli counter at the supermarket. Dribble the fig and the cheese generously with your favorite honey and tuck in. I have been known to squash both the ricotta and the fig with a fork onto some buttered toast—tuck into that as well, it's all good stuff.

## beefsteak tomatoes, basil, ham and mild cheese on thick toast

This is something my dad used to make me on holidays in Cyprus from the hotel's self-service breakfast bar. I've finally found a purpose for the good old beefsteak tomato—for this recipe they are fantastic.

This brekkie or snack takes precisely one minute to make. So in go two slices of thick bread to the toaster. While toasting, you need to slice your tomatoes as thick as you like, get out a couple of small sprigs of basil, some sliced ham, which I like to remove the fat from, and some mild cheese. Out comes your hot toast. Place it on a plate and very lightly rub it with a garlic clove sliced in half (it's a gesture and it's breakfast, so don't go over the top but it's well worth doing). Then drizzle with some good olive oil—you could butter it if you fancy but I think olive oil keeps in with the Mediterranean thing. Then simply place on your tomatoes—very important, season now with sea salt and freshly ground black pepper. Rip over your basil. Lay on your ham and cheese and tuck in. Very simple, very tasty.

P.S. A nice poached free-range egg on top does the trick if you've got the extra time.

# pukkolla

Pukkolla is my name for this outrageously scrumptious concoction. It's one of the best things you can have for breakfast as it's got everything you need to kickstart your day. Basically it's a bastardized, personally composed muesli. The great thing about it is that you can adjust it to your own preference. It's very handy to have a large plastic airtight container to store your composed pukkolla in, so try and get hold of one.

## composing and preserving

*serves many mornings*
8 large handfuls of organic rolled oats
2 large handfuls of ground bran
1 handful of chopped dried apricots
1 handful of chopped dried dates
1 handful of crumbled walnuts
1 handful of smashed or chopped almonds, hazelnuts or Brazil nuts

Add your oats and bran to your plastic container with the apricots and dates. Add the walnuts and your other chosen nuts (I usually bash them up in a dishtowel). At this point feel free to improvise, adding any other preferred dried fruits like raisins, sultanas or figs—but personally I think my combination works pretty well. This will keep for a good couple of months very happily in your airtight container, but you'll have eaten it by then, I guarantee.

## making and knocking together

milk to cover
$1/2$ crunchy apple per person, washed and unpeeled

I would definitely try to make this the night or day before you want to eat it, although it can be made at the time (but you won't get the smooth silky scrumptious texture that the milk gives it overnight). I normally place double the amount of composed pukkolla cereal I need (i.e., four portions for two people) into a bowl. Doubling up like this gives you enough to eat for the next couple of days. Cover with milk, grate in around $1/2$ an apple per person and stir immediately to keep the apple from discoloring. Place in the fridge.

## tucking in and eating

¹/₂ banana per person, peeled and sliced, or mashed
honey to taste

Remove the bowl from the fridge. You will find that it has softened and thickened, so loosen with a little milk. Add your banana, sliced or mashed. You will find that a lot of natural sweetness has come out of the dried fruit, so add honey to taste. Serve in a bowl with a dollop of yogurt and some mixed fresh berries.

# homemade yogurt

I love making yogurt. For some reason it's really rewarding, I'm not sure why. I think it's the fact that it's so damn easy to turn 2 pints of milk into 2 pints of yogurt. Things like yogurt and bread are fantastic for kids to make, so let them have a go. Use natural yogurt, with acidophilus and other live culture.

4½ cups whole milk, preferably organic
One 16-oz container plain, natural yogurt

Bring your milk to the boil in a thick-bottomed pan, then turn the heat off. Leave for around 40 minutes until the milk has cooled down to body temperature. Use your finger to check. At this point stir or whisk in the yogurt. Cover and leave at room temperature for 6–8 hours, by which time you'll be amazed to see that the milk has turned into creamy yogurt. Without getting too technical, the live culture in the yogurt turns the natural sugar of the milk into acid. This causes the milk to thicken and taste slightly sharp. Different yogurts may react slightly differently, i.e., some will thicken more than others, but, as a rule, all results are fantastic. Place it in the fridge to chill. It will keep for around a week.

Here are some of my favorite ways to eat yogurt for breakfast or dessert, but don't forget it's great in marinades (see page 194) and fantastically refreshing lobbed over spicy lamb and couscous or curry and rice:

- With vanilla sugar
- With strawberries marinated in balsamic vinegar
- With mixed soft fruit
- With rosewater, honey and pistachio nuts
- With pukkolla (see page 32)
- With figs and a bit of brandy
- With baked fruit

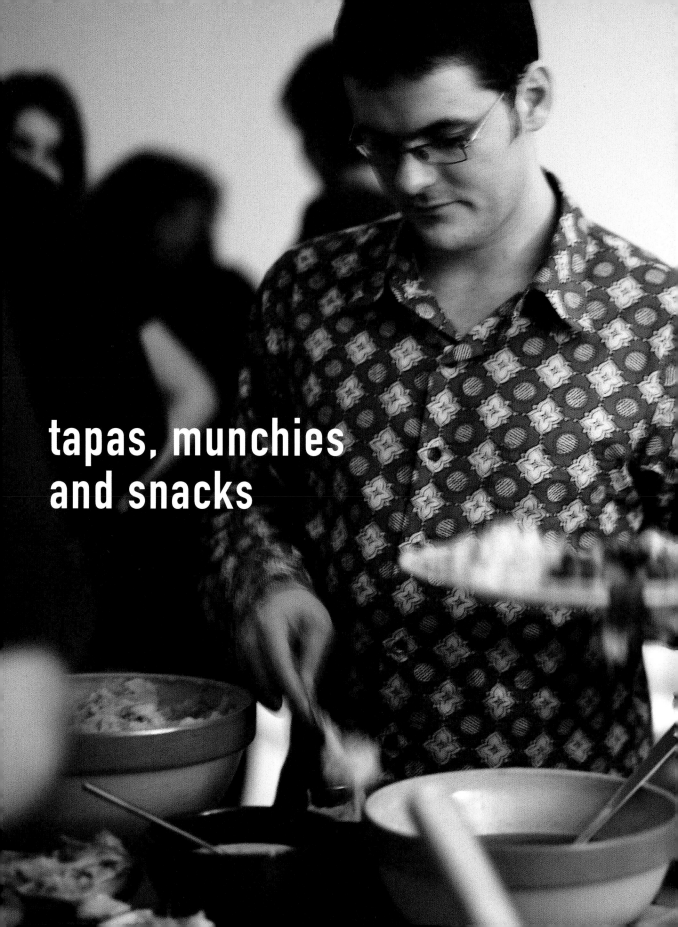

# tapas, munchies
# and snacks

I'm a right one for munchies and snacks, and the whole tapas thing really gets me going. I must admit I love the old Boxing Day (the day after Christmas) dinner so much that I do constantly try and reenact it for the rest of the year with the snacks in this chapter. My missus, sorry, the lovely Jules, often finds me watching telly late at night after work or a band practice gnawing on some stale old bread, pickled chillies and various other preserved or recycled dinners. She always looks disgusted by my new and innovative combinations but sod it, I'm happy.

When having friends over for drinks, or if people just pop round, it's fantastic to offer them a little nibble of something. If you've got a couple of simple tricks up your sleeve they'll think you're a right little tiger and that you've made a bit of an effort for them. If you're a bit of a midnight muncher like me, then check out this chapter for some finger-, bite- and snack-sized tucker.

Any combination of dishes in this chapter works extremely well but personally I like to serve them with some interesting homemade bread. Try my flat breads (pages 235–6), as they will go brilliantly with everything in this chapter.

## pan-toasted almonds with a touch of chilli and sea salt

These must be the quickest thing in the world to make. Believe me, there's nothing more scrumptious with any cold drink and good company than a plate of hot, toasted, tasty almonds. Try throwing them into salads too—nothing better.

*serves 8*
1/2 tablespoon olive oil
9oz shelled and peeled almonds
1–3 small dried red chillies
2 generous pinches of sea salt

Add the olive oil and almonds to a hot frying pan. Fry and kinda toast the almonds until golden brown, shaking the pan regularly to color them evenly and accentuate their nutty flavor. Crumble in the chilli to taste and add the sea salt. Toss over and serve hot on a large plate. Bloomin' gorgeous.

tapas, munchies and snacks

# smashed spiced chickpeas

This is a bastardized hummus recipe, but no less tasty. I love it best smeared over thin pizza crusts (see page 232) cooked on a hot griddle until charred, but tortillas are always a quick option.

*serves 6*
one 14-oz can of chickpeas or use 6oz dried ones,
    soaked and cooked until tender
a good pinch of cumin seeds, pounded
1–2 small dried red chillies, crumbled
1 clove of garlic, peeled and pounded to a paste
juice of 1 lemon
salt and freshly ground black pepper
extra-virgin olive oil

This is so simple to make. Really it's all about personal taste—the way I look at it is that chickpeas need a good kick up the backside to really get their flavors happening. So by smashing them up and adding a good pinch of cumin for a bit of spice, a little dried chilli for a touch of heat, garlic for a bit of ooorrrggghhh, a good squeezing of lemon juice to give it a twang and seasoning to taste, you pretty much hit the nail on the head. Then add extra-virgin olive oil to loosen and flavor. Love it.

# black olive tapenade

Olives with pits in are much tastier—they will make all the difference to this tapenade.

*serves 6–8*
9oz black olives, pitted
1 clove of garlic, peeled
6 anchovy fillets
salt and freshly ground black pepper
extra-virgin olive oil
juice of 1 lemon

Pit the olives by squeezing or bashing them and removing the pit. You can either very finely chop the olives, garlic and anchovies by hand or place them in a food processor and whizz until smooth. Correct the seasoning, add olive oil to loosen and, very important, add lemon juice to taste.

# blackened sweet eggplant

Some people call this "poor man's caviar" but I say it's "Essex boy's caviar."

*serves 6–8*
4 firm eggplants
a pinch of cumin seeds, pounded
1 clove of garlic, pounded to a paste
extra-virgin olive oil
juice of 2 or 3 lemons, to taste
salt and freshly ground black pepper
1 handful of fresh cilantro, basil or parsley, chopped (optional)

Preheat the oven to its hottest setting. Place the eggplants in a roasting pan and cook for 1 hour, until the insides are very soft. Remove from the oven, slit the skin and scrape out the insides. Add your cumin and garlic, stir in and break up. You can make this smooth or coarse, depending on how you feel. Add olive oil to loosen. Squeeze in your lemon juice and season to taste. I would never serve this hot, but it's great just warm or at room temperature. If adding herbs do this at the last minute, roughly or finely chopped.

# smashed zucchini paste

This is fantastic spread over toasted breads, thrown into pasta or even in ravioli with ricotta. Try to buy small firm zucchini, as they have a better flavor and are not all soft and fluffy in the middle.

*serves 6–8*
extra-virgin olive oil
2 cloves of garlic, peeled and finely chopped
1–2 small dried red chillies, crumbled
6–8 small zucchini, unevenly sliced
salt and freshly ground black pepper
1 good handful of fresh mint, chopped
juice of 1 lemon

Put a couple of glugs of oil in a hot pan and fry your garlic and chillies for a couple of minutes. Throw in the zucchini, stir around and coat. Turn the heat down slightly and put the lid on. Give the pan a shake and stir every 5 minutes for around 35 minutes, making sure the zucchini don't stick to the bottom. Cooking with the lid on will ensure that there's a little moisture in the pan. When the zucchini are really soft, with some chunky pieces and the rest almost pulped, remove from the heat and taste carefully. Remembering that this will probably be used on bread, you may have to adjust the chilli to your taste. Season well and pour in 4 good glugs of extra-virgin olive oil to flavor and loosen. Finally add your chopped mint and lemon juice.

# marinated olives

The thing about olives is that there are so many varieties, so when at deli counters in supermarkets, feel free to ask to try all of them. When I've found a type I like, I buy around 1lb each time. The olives can then be flavored with fantastic things—but use dried flavorings if you want the olives to keep well.

Mix your olives in a bowl with a good sprinkling of dried oregano, a ripped-up bay leaf and some crumbled dried red chillies. Season with just pepper, as olives are salty already, and add some cracked coriander seeds or fennel seeds. Then pack the olives tightly into an airtight jar and cover with a good olive oil. This is a fantastic marinade which will complement your olives, making them dead tasty and great for cooking with, using in salads or simply as finger food with drinks.

# blackened marinated peppers

Fantastic as part of a tapas or antipasti selection, or serve simply with a piece of grilled fish or in salads.

*serves 6*
4 large bell peppers (2 red, 2 yellow)
1 large clove of garlic, peeled and finely sliced
1–2 small dried red chillies, crumbled
1 tablespoon coriander seeds
5 good glugs of extra-virgin olive oil
a splash of red wine vinegar
salt and freshly ground black pepper
1 good handful of fresh basil

Normally I place the peppers directly on the gas flame. This can also be done on a grill or under the broiler. Once blackened all over, allow to steam in a covered bowl for 5 minutes. Peel and seed. Don't wash the skins off under running water, as you will lose a little of the fantastic sweetness that you've created by blackening them. I normally tear each pepper into around 8 strips and place them in a bowl. Add the garlic, chillies, coriander seeds and olive oil to the peppers with a good splash of red wine vinegar. The key is to season well to taste. Toss this and, ideally, allow to sit for an hour, tossing occasionally, before ripping in your basil and serving.

# slow-cooked and stuffed baby cherry chilli peppers

These are the most fantastic thing. You eat the chillies whole and they are amazing as munchies with drinks, not too hot. At the same time they make lovely flavored olive oil, which I like to add garlic and bay to for extra flavor. Great used on salads, over mozzarella and other cheeses, on pizzas and over pasta.

*makes 10 portions*
2¼ lbs small, round baby red cherry chilli peppers
a medium-sized bottle of olive oil (don't panic—see below!)
1 good handful of fresh flat-leaf parsley or basil
2 good handfuls of argula
1 small handful of capers, soaked and drained
1 handful of anchovies
10 tablespoons balsamic vinegar, or enough to cover
salt and freshly ground black pepper

Halve your chillies, remove the seeds and wash in cold water. Then drain. Tightly pack into a large earthenware dish and cover with the olive oil, then place in a 325°F oven for 35–45 minutes until just tender. *Carefully* remove the dish from the oven and let it cool. Take the chillies out of the dish and set aside. Pour the fantastic flavored olive oil back into the bottle it came from. Finely chop your parsley or basil, arugula and capers. Roughly chop the anchovies and then mix everything up in a bowl. Just before you want to serve them, dress with the balsamic vinegar, and season. Stuff this filling into your chillies and serve on a plate as tapas.

## marinated anchovies

Unless you're lucky enough to get fresh ones, the best anchovies you can get hold of are nearly always salted and whole. These are still great for cooking, but to eat an anchovy like you do when abroad, draped over toasted crostini, with milky cheeses and in salads, I personally feel no matter how good the anchovy is, the salt overpowers the natural flavor of the dish. So what I do is marinate anchovies to remove their excess salt and then infuse them with other interesting flavors.

Simply take your anchovies off the bone and leave them under running water for a couple of minutes. Pat dry and place a layer snugly in a dish or on a plate. The main thing is to have something acidic to remove the salt, and a good sweet wine, lemon juice or herb vinegar will do this—add just enough to nearly cover the anchovies. Add the same amount of good olive oil and then any flavours that take your fancy, such as chilli, fennel seeds, fresh parsley, fresh thyme or flecks of garlic and lemon peel. To make all the difference, marinate in the fridge for 2–16 hours before eating.

## grilled butterflied sardines

*serves 6–8*
1 small handful of fresh bread crumbs
a pinch of dried oregano
1–2 small dried red chillies, crumbled
1 small handful of fresh flat-leaf parsley, chopped
peel of 1 lemon, finely chopped
salt and freshly ground black pepper
8 large fresh sardines, scaled and gutted

Mix everything, apart from the sardines, in a bowl, then remove the heads from the sardines. Open the belly of each fish. What you need to do is remove the spine and bones from the flesh. It's a bit fiddly, but well worth doing. With one hand you need to pinch away the flesh from the spine; with your other hand pull the spine away from the flesh. You will end up with the boned fillets butterflied open. Then all you have to do is press your flavored bread crumb mixture on each side of the sardines.

I like to cook the fish on a very hot ridged griddle pan or grill. Some of the bread crumb mix will fall off during cooking, but that doesn't matter because it will have imparted its flavor by then and done its job. It literally takes 1–2 minutes to cook until crisp. Serve on a plate with some halved lemons. Fantastic. Wicked with a glass of wine.

# marinated squid with chickpeas and chilli

*serves 6–8*
6 medium-sized squid, gutted and cleaned
One 14-oz can of chickpeas or use 6 oz dried ones,
    soaked and cooked until tender
1 small knob of fresh ginger, peeled and finely sliced
around 4 glugs of extra-virgin olive oil
juice of 2 lemons
2 fresh red chillies, seeded and finely sliced
salt and freshly ground black pepper
1 handful of fresh flat-leaf parsley, finely chopped
1 handful of fresh cilantro, torn

You can ask your fishmonger to clean the squid for you and score it in a crisscross pattern. This will allow your marinade to get right in there. In a hot griddle or frying pan, or over the grill, sear and char the squid. It should take about a minute for the white flesh and a little longer for the tentacles. Remove and slice the white flesh of each squid into 3 or 4 pieces, leaving the tentacles whole. Put the rest of the ingredients, except the herbs, into a bowl, then add your squid while still hot and toss everything together. Just before serving, throw in your herbs and check again for seasoning.

# salted and spiced shrimp

Basically what we are doing here is encrusting spicy salt onto the shrimp shells.

*serves 6–8*
2¼ lb small shrimp, uncooked and in the shell
4 generous pinches of sea salt
6 generous pinches of mixed spices (fennel, coriander, cumin, chilli), lightly crushed

Leave the shells on the shrimp, although you can remove the heads if you want. Get a wok or large pan very hot, then add the salt and spices. Toast and toss around for 30 seconds before adding your shrimp. Shake vigorously and toss. Your salt and spices will stick and encrust themselves to the shrimp. After a minute or two the shrimp will have cooked and changed color and should be tasty and crunchy. I normally eat the shells but you don't have to.

# Asian-infused tuna

Try to buy firm, deep-red tuna. The idea is for it to be eaten raw—just like sushi—but, in actual fact, the acidity of the lime juice starts to cook the fish.

*serves 6–8*

1lb tuna, bluefin if possible

1 ripe avocado, peeled and diced

juice of 4–5 limes, to taste

1–2 fresh chillies, seeded and finely chopped

3 tablespoons sesame seed oil

4 tablespoons coconut milk

1 good handful of fresh cilantro, finely chopped

2 heaped tablespoons sesame seeds

a little fresh ginger, peeled and finely chopped

soy sauce, to taste

Finely dice your tuna and place in a bowl. Add the rest of the ingredients, stir and add soy sauce to season. This fantastically flavored tuna is great on thinly sliced toasted bread.

# simple salads and dressings

I love salads and, like in the last book, I've made them really simple and conversational. Try to eat salads regularly and you'll really get into them. I've spoken to so many people about what they like to eat, and you won't be surprised that most blokes when asked what they like say "MEAT," "MEAT AND TWO VEG"—that means French fries and mashed potatoes. Well, that's great—me too. But you can't beat a good salad. Even when I'm taken out to some of the most expensive restaurants in London I still always ask for the chef's mixed salad even if it's not on the menu. I think it tells you a lot about a kitchen when you order a salad—you will either get one that has been chucked together without much thought or you will get a mixture of fantastic different greens and herbs which, when eaten, makes you think, "God, that's nice. What was that I just ate?" A great salad can also simply be one or two things that complement each other. It doesn't have to be complicated.

So to get friendly with salads you should buy a couple of nice big salad bowls that you can put in the middle of the table, acquire some good extra-virgin olive oil, some different vinegars—there's so much choice now—and buy some things that you have never thought of trying before. There's loads of new salad greens, different types of radishes and tomatoes, etc. It's endless. Get stuck in.

# mozzarella and grilled chilli salad

Another great salad that can get away with being part of an antipasto selection as well as a main course salad or sandwich filling. Simple flavors again: it's all based around the milky soft mozzarella and the slightly more refined heat of the grilled chilli. If possible try to buy buffalo mozzarella, as it's made out of buffalo milk which makes the cheese far more tasty and delicate in both texture and taste. The salad doesn't work nearly as well with that chewy horrible stuff that is used on pizzas.

I normally use 1 fresh red chilli to every ball of mozzarella, but do use more or less as you please. Prick the chillies with a knife, otherwise they can puff up and explode in your face, and place them straight onto the flame if you have a gas stove. If you don't have gas, put them in a pan on the highest setting of your electric stove. Both ways you need to blacken the chillies on all sides, so turn when need be. When fully blackened, place in a sandwich bag, wrap in plastic wrap or cover in a bowl for 5 minutes, until cool. This will steam the skins and make peeling and seeding easier.

While the chillies are steaming, gently rip up your mozzarella into 4 or 5 pieces and randomly place on a large plate. Peel and seed the chillies and slice lengthwise as thinly as you like. It's quite important to scatter them evenly over the mozzarella and very important to wash your hands after doing so before you rub your eyes or anything else! Now rip up some purple and green basil over the top, and sprinkle with sea salt and freshly ground black pepper. Add a little squeeze of lemon juice and a generous glug of olive oil. Nice one.

## squashed cherry tomato and smashed olive salad

This is probably the quickest salad I make, but no less tasty for that. Very few ingredients, simple flavors, complete sense. Try to make use of the wider range of cherry tomatoes available now: yellow, striped and grape cherry tomatoes for instance. And, as I always say, it's much better, tastewise, to buy olives with their pits still in than without. Trust me.

Always going along the line of 4 parts tomatoes to 1 part olives, simply squash your tomatoes into a bowl. I always have to put one hand over the tomatoes as I do this as juice and seeds go everywhere—generally on me. You can be as rough with the tomatoes as you like, as the salad looks much better rough and rustic than perfect and pretty. Then gently smash the olives on a board with a hard object—a cup or a rolling pin. Remove the pits, throw the olives in with the tomatoes and toss together.

That's the basis of the salad made now, but what you've done already makes complete sense in cooking. Tomatoes need salt, olives are preserved in salt, you've squeezed the juice out of the tomatoes, which in turn draws the salt and the smoky flavor out of the olives. This makes the olives very edible and the tomatoes damn tasty. That's the most important bit done; all we can do now is enhance it. This can be done to your personal taste with a couple of dribbles of vinegar, preferably red wine or herb, some freshly ground black pepper and 2 or 3 good glugs of olive oil. And just before serving, rip in as much basil as you can afford and even a handful of arugula if you have some. Lovely.

P.S. If you have any leftovers, then toss them in with some hot spaghetti.

# couscous with grilled summer vegetables and loadsa herbs

This couscous recipe is quite a bit different from the norm because instead of boiling or steaming the couscous you just dress it raw with a really tasty dressing. This means it keeps a slight bite which I think is more interesting for a salad.

*serves 4*
9oz couscous
1 1/3 cups cold water
3 red bell peppers
1 handful of asparagus, trimmed and peeled if need be
2 or 3 small firm zucchini or patty pan squash, sliced
1 small bunch of scallions, trimmed and finely sliced
2–4 fresh red chillies, seeded and finely sliced
3 good handfuls of mixed fresh herbs (basil, cilantro, mint,
    flat-leaf parsley)
2 olive oil and lemon juice dressing recipes (page 81)
salt and freshly ground black pepper
red wine vinegar

Place the couscous in a bowl with the cold water. This will start to soften the couscous and you will see the water disappear as it soaks in. While the couscous is softening, we need to blacken the peppers. I do this by placing the peppers directly onto the flame of my gas stove. If you don't have gas, then blacken under the broiler. Both ways you need to blacken the peppers on all sides, so turn when need be. When fully blackened, place in a sandwich bag, wrap in plastic wrap or cover in a bowl for 5 minutes, until cool. This will steam the skins and make peeling and seeding easier. Remove the skins and seeds and roughly chop.

On a very hot ridged skillet, lightly char the asparagus and squash on both sides, then toss them into the bowl of couscous with the peppers, scallions, chillies and ripped-up herbs. Mix well. Add the olive oil and lemon juice dressing and toss well. Finally, taste and season with salt and pepper and a couple of dribbles of red wine vinegar for a slight twang. It's a beautiful thing.

# warm salad of winter greens, bacon and Jerusalem artichokes

As far as salads go, this is a real hearty one, full of flavor and pretty damn gutsy. The idea behind warm salads is that you have interesting and slightly more robust salad leaves, usually mixed with sautéed vegetables or roasted meat. Anything from chicken livers, bacon and scallops to roasted tomatoes, pine nuts and caramelized onions, anything really. Bacon and Jerusalem artichokes is a brilliant combination.

Jerusalem artichokes are becoming more common in supermarkets now, but don't confuse them with globe artichokes, which look like big fat thistles. Jerusalem artichokes look more like new potatoes gone mad. For this recipe I normally use around 2 artichokes and 2 strips of bacon per person, but it really is up to you. I also use any combination of radicchio, romaine, oak leaf, curly endive, arugula and baby spinach.

Rip the greens up and place in a salad bowl or on a plate. I prefer to scrub the Jerusalem artichokes instead of peeling them, before cooking in salted boiling water until just soft. Cool under cold running water, drain, and slice as you would sautéed potatoes. Then in a large frying pan fry some dry-cured bacon, which should be sliced across as thick as you like. When golden crisp, remove from the pan and put to one side. Add your sliced artichokes to the pan with a small glug of oil, a little butter and some salt and freshly ground black pepper. Shake the pan occasionally, adding the bacon back into the pan when the artichokes are also golden and crisp. Sprinkle over the salad greens and drizzle generously with either the basil and balsamic vinegar dressing (page 80) or the mustard and herb vinegar dressing (page 81).

## watercress, arugula, sweet pear, walnut and Parmesan salad

What a pukka combination, simple and classy. Don't try to make
this when you feel like it, make it when you can buy perfect pears,
otherwise it will taste naff. For one person I normally use
around half a pear, 2 big handfuls of watercress and 2 big
handfuls of arugula. If the pear skins are nice I just give
them a wash, if not I remove them with a peeler. Then cut
them in half and remove the core. It doesn't really matter

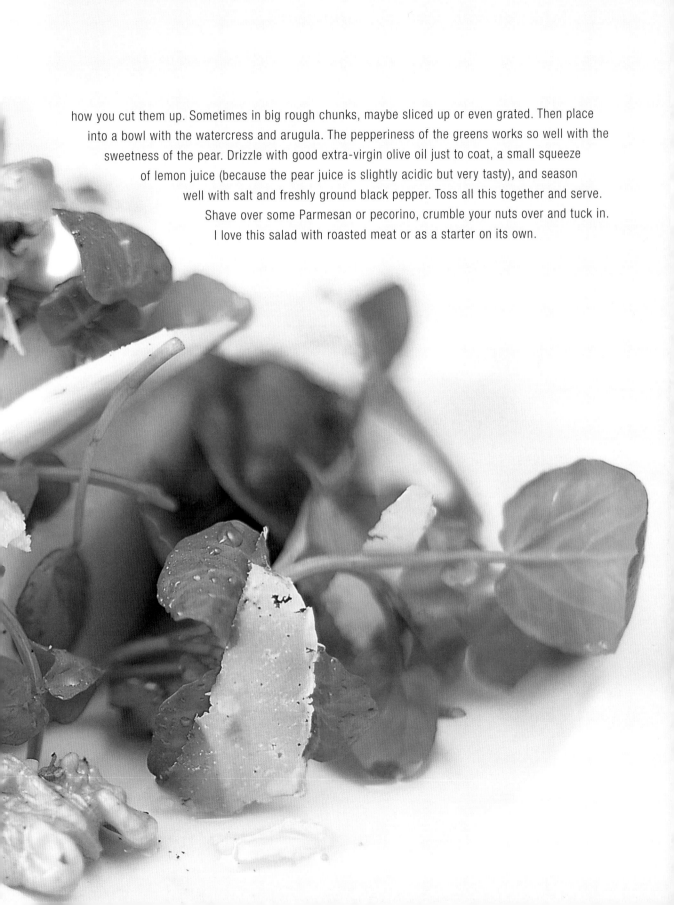

how you cut them up. Sometimes in big rough chunks, maybe sliced up or even grated. Then place
into a bowl with the watercress and arugula. The pepperiness of the greens works so well with the
sweetness of the pear. Drizzle with good extra-virgin olive oil just to coat, a small squeeze
of lemon juice (because the pear juice is slightly acidic but very tasty), and season
well with salt and freshly ground black pepper. Toss all this together and serve.
Shave over some Parmesan or pecorino, crumble your nuts over and tuck in.
I love this salad with roasted meat or as a starter on its own.

## crunchy Thai salad

The thing I love about this salad is that it's so crunchy and tasty and you just know that it's really really good for you. Any combination of the following ingredients is great: sprouts, finely sliced green and red bell peppers, baby spinach, finely sliced and seeded red or green chillies, arugula, sliced scallions, peeled, gutted and sliced cucumbers, finely sliced Chinese or Savoy cabbage, whole sugar snap peas and fresh herbs like mint, basil and cilantro. Dress with the Thai dressing on page 80. Then sprinkle with some lightly toasted cashews or sesame seeds. Fantastic. If you want to make this more substantial, then toss in some cooked and chilled egg noodles.

## mixed greens salad with mozzarella, mint, peach and prosciutto

Try to get hold of buffalo mozzarella. I like to crumble a little bit of dried chilli over my mozzarella, but I'm a chilli freak and you may not be, so you don't have to! And use any mixed greens you fancy.

If I make this for my lunch I'll use one nice, ripe peach, a ball of mozzarella and a couple of slices of prosciutto. Pinch the skin and peel from the bottom to the top, then quarter the peaches. Rip the mozzarella into small pieces and place on a plate with the peaches. Lightly season. Lay a couple of slices of prosciutto over the top. Dress your mixed salad greens and torn-up mint with a little of the olive oil and lemon juice dressing (page 81). Throw the greens on top of the plate.

# salad of boiled potatoes, avocado and mustard cress

I had to do this salad, even though mustard cress must be one of the tackiest things in the world. For some reason I'm absolutely addicted to it and love it to bits. This is my favorite combination.

*serves 4–6*
1 ½lb scrubbed new potatoes
1 large ripe avocado
3 good handfuls of mustard cress, washed
olive oil
juice of 1–2 lemons
salt and freshly ground black pepper

Cook the new potatoes in salted boiling water until very tender, then drain. Slice the avocado in half and remove the pit. Peel and slice it lengthwise into thick slices or chunks (however you like, really) and place in a bowl. Slice any large potatoes in half—this will expose their flesh to the olive oil and lemon juice. If they are small, leave them whole. Add to the bowl. Throw the mustard cress in, then add a couple of good glugs of olive oil and lemon juice to taste. Season and toss. Serve on a big plate, scattered with any remaining mustard cress. This is brilliant with chicken, fish or as a salad on its own, especially in the summer.

## salad of marinated charred squid with cannellini beans, arugula and chilli

*serves 4–6*
2¼lb squid, trimmed and gutted
salt and freshly ground black pepper
One 14-oz can of cannellini beans, or use 6 oz dried ones,
    soaked and cooked until tender
1–2 fresh chillies, red and green
2 good handfuls of arugula
juice of 2 limes or 1 lemon
olive oil
extra-virgin olive oil

Try to get your fishmonger to skin and gut your squid for you. Score the squid lightly in a casual crisscross fashion. Set it to one side while you get a skillet very very hot. You can also use a wok or the grill. Season the squid lightly just before cooking, then add it to the pan. After a minute it should be nicely charred, so turn it over and cook for a further minute, then remove it and put it aside. Heat up the cannellini beans and sprinkle them into a bowl. Add the sliced chillies to the bowl with the arugula, lime or lemon juice and olive oil, and season. Cut the squid at irregular angles and toss it in with the rest of the ingredients. A good drizzle of extra-virgin olive oil over the top will finish it off nicely.

## celery, celeriac, parsley and pomegranate salad

This is a really clean salad, fantastic with fish or cold meats. For it to be as delicate as it should be, the celery and celeriac should be very finely sliced. You can do this by hand with a knife or with a mandolin slicer, which you can pick up really cheaply. It will make the job so much easier. I normally use 1 whole celeriac to 1 head of celery.

All you have to do is strip back the celery and peel the celeriac and then finely slice. Place in a bowl with some chopped flat-leaf parsley and a handful of pomegranate seeds (make sure you use just the red seeds, not the bitter yellow stuff). Season and dress with olive oil and lemon juice dressing (page 81). This salad can be dressed a little before you need it, as opposed to at the table. Place on a large plate and sprinkle with some extra pomegranate seeds. Sometimes I crumble goat's cheese over this, or some ricotta which I encrust with dried herbs, salt and pepper, drizzled with olive oil and baked until golden in a hot oven.

# dressings

Talk about simple things making me happy. Why is it a 24-year-old boy thinks he's really clever just by making his dressings in a jam jar? I feel like a bit of a trainspotter really. It sounds almost too simple but, the fact is, we all end up with empty jam jars. Just chuck all your dressing ingredients into a jam jar, tighten the lid and shake up. Dress your salad, and any leftovers can remain in the jar, in the back of the fridge, raring to dress your next salad. And the best thing is that there's no washing up of bowls, whisks and bottles, just a jam jar.

I've found that the vinegar-based dressings will taste great for a week or so, but the dressings with lemon or lime juice or dairy products in them will only taste good for a couple of days. On pages 80–81 you will find 6 tasty and simple dressings. Each will make enough to dress a salad for 4 people, but feel free to double the amounts if you need more.

## basil, balsamic vinegar and pine nut dressing

2 tablespoons balsamic vinegar

5 tablespoons extra-virgin olive oil

1 good handful of chopped fresh basil

1 good handful of pine nuts, toasted and chopped

salt and freshly ground black pepper, to taste


## cilantro and crème fraîche dressing

3 tablespoons extra-virgin olive oil

3 tablespoons crème fraîche

3 teaspoons Dijon mustard

2–3 tablespoons fresh lemon juice

2 handfuls of fresh cilantro, pounded or finely chopped

salt and freshly ground black pepper, to taste


## Thai dressing

4 tablespoons fresh lime juice

3 tablespoons olive oil

1 tablespoon sesame seed oil

1 tablespoon soy sauce

a good pinch of brown sugar

1 tablespoon fresh ginger, peeled and finely chopped

1/2 clove of garlic, finely sliced

1 fresh red chilli, seeded and finely sliced

1 large handful of fresh cilantro and basil, chopped

## mustard and herb vinegar dressing

6 tablespoons olive oil

2 tablespoons Dijon mustard

2 tablespoons red or white wine herb vinegar

1 level teaspoon salt

1 teaspoon freshly ground black pepper


## olive oil and lemon juice dressing

2 tablespoons fresh lemon juice

5 tablespoons olive oil

salt and freshly ground black pepper, to taste


## sweet cherry tomato dressing

1 teacup of ripe, washed cherry tomatoes, finely chopped

$1/2$ clove of garlic, finely sliced

6 tablespoons olive oil

2 tablespoons red wine vinegar

1 handful of basil, pounded or finely chopped

a pinch of dried red pepper flakes

salt and freshly ground black pepper, to taste

2 anchovy fillets, chopped (optional)

**soups and broths**

Good soups are fantastic comfort food. They're dead simple to make, but the most important thing to remember is that you must use good stock. Now before you start thinking you're going to have to be boiling things for hours, let me tell you what stock is to me at home. It's Sunday night, we've had roast chicken with all the trimmings for dinner and now I'm washing up. Two things can happen: one, I can pick up the remains of the chicken and chuck them in the garbage; or two, I can throw the remains into a pot with some root veg (carrots, onions, celery and some sprigs of herbs from the windowbox), cover with water, then bring to the boil and simmer for an hour. There you go, fantastic tasty simple stock. I usually strain it before putting it in containers and freezing it, where it just sits waiting to be used for sauces, gravy or soups. Easy peasy. Not a bouillon cube in sight. If you're vegetarian, then great stocks can still be made with lots of fresh vegetables—most important, use a handful of dried mushrooms, as these will give the stock a really substantial flavor. You'll find three stock recipes on pages 275–6.

# potato and Jerusalem artichoke soup with thyme, mascarpone and hazelnuts

*serves 4–6*

2 large pats of butter

2 cloves of garlic, finely chopped

1 onion, finely chopped

1lb Jerusalem artichokes, peeled and chopped

8oz potatoes, peeled and chopped

1 good handful of fresh thyme leaves, picked off stems

5 cups chicken or vegetable stock (pages 275–6)

5$\frac{1}{2}$oz mascarpone cheese

salt and freshly ground black pepper

7oz hazelnuts, toasted and broken up

In a large pan, melt the butter and slowly fry the garlic, onion, artichokes, potatoes and thyme. Add the stock, then bring to the boil and simmer for about 30 minutes, until the potatoes and artichokes are tender. Blend in a blender or food processor just enough to leave it chunky or blend until a smooth purée. Reheat, adding the mascarpone and the seasoning. Serve sprinkled with the hazelnuts.

# Mary's Saturday soup and dumplings

Mary is the mother of my mate Kevin and her Saturday soup is famous in east London. It's great comfort food that originates from the West Indies. There are tales behind its name but basically it's a chunky, robust soup that is supposed to use up any leftover vegetables. Who cares where its name comes from—it's bloody tasty, even on a Monday, and that's all that matters! I've changed Mary's recipe to suit my taste—I'll probably get a slap for it, but that's cooking and you can do what you like!

*serves 6–8*

*dumplings*

4 heaped tablespoons self-rising flour

4 heaped tablespoons cornmeal
   (if unavailable use all-purpose flour)

1/4 cup soft butter

salt and freshly ground black pepper

water to bind

*soup*

1 1/2lb stewing lamb or beef, diced

salt and freshly ground black pepper

olive oil

1 medium onion, finely sliced

1 medium carrot, roughly chopped

2 tablespoons coriander seeds

2 handfuls of fresh thyme

2 large yams, peeled and chopped into
   chunks

1 butternut squash (or 1lb pumpkin),
   peeled, seeded and chopped into
   chunks

1lb sweet potato, peeled and chopped into
   chunks

5 cups chicken stock (page 275)

One 14-oz can of coconut milk

9 oz okra

2–3 fresh red chillies, seeded
   and chopped

Rub together the flour, cornmeal, butter and seasoning, adding water bit by bit to form a stiff dough. Roll into balls slightly smaller than golf balls and put to one side.

In a large pot, fry the seasoned meat in a little olive oil until lightly colored. Add the onion, carrot, coriander seeds and thyme. Shake around and soften slightly before adding the yams, squash and sweet potatoes. Turn down the heat and cook for 20 minutes with the lid on, shaking regularly. Stir in the stock, lay the dumplings on top and simmer for 40 minutes with the lid on before adding the coconut milk and okra and cooking for a final 10 minutes. Carefully season, tasting as you go. Sprinkle with the chillies before serving. Scrummy.

P.S. Instead of throwing away the squash seeds, roast them in a little oil and salt until crisp. Serve either sprinkled over the soup or on their own with drinks.

# squash, Parma ham hock, sage, onion and barley broth

In Italy, when slicing Parma and prosciutto ham, the first half, which is really lean, is used in salads and meat plates. The next bit of the ham is fatty and more sinewy, lending itself to being wrapped around fish and meat and roasting. What's left of the ham is the hock, and this is great cooked slowly with beans or used in soups. In England we don't seem to cook much with hocks and I've found that in supermarkets they are either discarded or set aside. So ask at the deli or butcher counter if you can have one. You should pay half the price for the hock compared to the lean ham. If not, have a word with the manager. If you find you can't get hold of one, then a regular ham or bacon hock will work just as well.

*serves 4–6*
1 red onion, finely chopped
1 tablespoon coriander seeds, crushed
2 cloves of garlic, peeled and finely chopped
olive oil
1 butternut squash, peeled, seeded and roughly chopped
2 good handfuls of fresh sage
1 good handful of pearl barley
5 cups chicken or vegetable stock (pages 275–6)
1½lb Parma ham hock, skin removed
sea salt and freshly ground black pepper
extra-virgin olive oil

*optional*
1 handful of chestnuts, shelled
a pinch of dried chilli and a pinch of nutmeg

In a large pot slowly fry the onion, coriander seeds and garlic in a little olive oil until softened. Then add the squash, sage, chestnuts if you're using them and pearl barley. Stir in the stock and add your Parma ham hock. Bring to the boil, then simmer for 1½ hours. Remove the hock, discard the bone if there is one, then break the meat up into small pieces with two forks and leave to one side. Take half the soup and liquidize it to make it smooth. Add it back to the pan with your broken-up ham, then season carefully with sea salt and freshly ground black pepper. Add a bit of chilli and ground nutmeg if you like, to taste. Feel free to loosen with a little extra stock if need be. Serve in a bowl with a little peppery extra-virgin olive oil and some hot crusty bread.

# seafood broth, ripped herbs, toasted bread and garlic aïoli

This broth is such a cracker. If a friend served this to me I'd be well impressed. Try it—you'll love it. I base it around mussels because they're tasty and a damn good value. You can add any other seafood you like. The aïoli is not essential with this, but it is fantastic and you should give it a go.

*serves 6*
1¾lb mixed seafood (squid, red mullet, shrimp and monkfish)
1¾lb mussels
One 14-oz can of plum tomatoes or 8 large ripe plum tomatoes
extra-virgin olive oil
2 cloves of garlic, peeled and sliced
2–3 fresh red chillies, seeded and sliced
2 good handfuls of zucchini, finely sliced
2 large glasses of dry white wine
salt and freshly ground black pepper
2 good handfuls of mixed fresh herbs, ripped
    (basil, parsley, fennel, marjoram)
garlic aïoli (page 276)
1 lemon

First clean up your seafood. I normally get my fishmonger to scale, gut and fillet the fish and clean the squid for me—it saves making a mess. Then all I have to do is pull the beards off the mussels. If using fresh tomatoes, remove their cores and place in boiling water for 1 minute—this will loosen their skins—then rinse quickly under cold water and remove the skins.

Into a very hot pan swiftly pour 4 good glugs of extra-virgin olive oil and add the mussels. Flick the garlic, chillies and zucchini on top, shake the pan around, then add the white wine. While this is sizzling away, really squash in the tomatoes and lay your mixed seafood on top. Turn the heat right down and simmer for around 5 minutes, until all the shellfish are open. Discard any that remain closed. Season with salt and freshly ground black pepper and add your herbs. Serve the broth in big bowls over some toasted bread and, if you want to make it really pukka, add a big lob of garlic aïoli on top and a wedge of lemon.

# fragrant Thai broth

This is a really satisfying and almost cleansing soup. It's easy to vary this broth by using different seafood or herbs and even by adding noodles to make it more substantial. It's quite classic to have finely sliced fried onions sprinkled on top just before serving—nice idea, but another pan to wash up!

*serves 4*
3 stalks of lemongrass, crushed and bruised
2 knobs of ginger, peeled, crushed and bruised
6 kaffir lime leaves, ripped up
5 cups chicken stock (page 275)
1–2 heaped tablespoons sugar
around 4–6 tablespoons fish sauce *(nam pla)*, to taste
juice of 1–2 limes
2 or 3 large shrimp per person, shelled, deveined and butterflied
1 good handful of fresh cilantro and basil

*garnish*
2 fresh chillies, sliced
1 red pepper, finely sliced
4 scallions, finely sliced

In a pestle and mortar bash together the lemon grass, ginger and lime leaves. Place in a pot with the stock, bring to the boil, then simmer for 10 minutes. Taste—it should be tasty and fragrant, but slightly bland. So add the sugar, fish sauce and lime juice to taste. What you are trying to achieve with these 3 ingredients is a slightly sweet, sour, salty and savory balance—but, to be honest, this is a personal thing, so add them bit by bit and keep tasting until you have a flavor you're happy with.

Now add the shrimp to the broth and cook for 1 minute. Remove the shrimp and divide them among 4 bowls, topped with the fresh herbs and garnish. You can now finish the soup by pouring your broth into each bowl. I like a bit of drama so I pour the broth into my glass Bodum teapot, plunging the fresh herbs into it. Visually this looks great but infusing the perfume from the herbs at the last minute like this also gives you a fresh and vibrant flavor. Feel free to improvise on the herbs—you don't have to stick to cilantro and basil.

gennaro

pasta and risotto

If you can crack one of these two, then your mates are gonna think you're a bit clever. A good pasta dish or a good risotto just can't be beaten. We're not talking about flashy food, we're talking about something really tasty, something mouth-watering and something with a real personal touch just waiting to be eaten—that's what it's all about, whether you're in a restaurant, sitting down with your family or having a dinner party. Give 'em a try.

In this chapter you'll find amazingly quick dried pasta recipes, as well as some gutsy homemade fresh pasta for all occasions and seasons. The basic risotto recipe is fantastic, giving you the perfect creamy base with some extremely simple variations—try them all and make up some of your own too.

## fresh pasta

Being able to make good fresh pasta is in my eyes one of the best things I've ever learned in cooking. It allows you to put character into the pasta as well as into the sauce, making snacks, lunches, dinners and dinner parties damn handsome and wholesome. And people can tell it's homemade and just love it. You've got to try it— it will be a real asset to your repertoire. The basic pasta recipe on the next page can be made in an electric mixer or food processor but I prefer doing it by hand so I can feel what's happening as I work the dough. Remember: save the egg whites that you're not using to make batters and meringues.

# blinding pasta recipe

*serves 4*
1 ²/₃ cups bread flour
1 ²/₃ cups semolina flour (if unavailable, bread flour will do)
3 large eggs
8 egg yolks

Place both flours on a clean surface. Make a well in the center and add the eggs and yolks. With a fork break up the eggs as you bring in the flour. Stir with the fork until you have a dough which you can work with your hands. Knead well until you have a smooth, silky and elastic dough and a clean surface. Wrap the dough in plastic wrap and rest it in the fridge for a while.

I use a pasta machine to roll out my pasta into thin sheets about 4 inches wide. Try to get one—they're great. They rarely break and only set you back about $40. However, you can use a rolling pin—it just takes a little longer to get the pasta as thin. Divide your ball of pasta into 4 pieces and keep covered. Working with one ball at a time, flatten out with your hand and run through the thickest setting on your machine. Fold in half and repeat this process several times, to give you perfect, textured pasta. Dust the sheet of pasta on both sides with flour before running it through the settings— I usually repeat this 4 or 5 times, dusting and moving the setting in each time until I have the desired thickness (normally about 1–2 mm thick, depending on the type of pasta I am making). It does take practice, but once you've cracked it, you'll be knocking out pasta like no one's business. It's all about coming to grips with how pasta works. It will stay fresh in the fridge for half a day or it can be dried (see page 101) and stored in airtight containers.

# shaping pasta from a sheet

So you've got your pasta sheets in front of you—now all you have to do is shape them. Check out the recipes on pages 103–23 using stracci, pappardelle, tagliatelle, ravioli and tortellini. There are so many things you can make by simply cutting, folding or filling pasta, so what are you waiting for? Get cracking.

# drying pasta

I generally make fresh pasta at home on special occasions or when friends are coming round. Saying that, I always tend to double or triple the recipe, making much more than I need, and I dry the rest, cutting it into any shape or size—this is great because it means I then have a supply of homemade pasta to last me, normally, a couple of weeks until the next time I make pasta. Superb.

To dry it, all you need to do is place the pasta on a rack or hang it on a coathanger or something similar for 1 or 2 days until completely dry. To test, scrunch a piece in your hand and it should crumble and snap into small brittle pieces quite easily. Dried pasta can be stored in airtight containers for a good couple of months once dried properly.

# stracci

Stracci basically means "ripped" or "ragged," and I love it because you can slice and rip the sheets of pasta as you like. Cut your pieces into varied shapes and sizes with different angles and lengths (see picture on page 104). Go for interesting shapes.

## stracci, spicy eggplant, tomatoes, basil and Parmesan

*serves 4*
1 large eggplant, cut into $1/2$-inch dice
1 teaspoon coriander seeds, cracked
1–2 dried red chillies, crumbled
olive oil
one 14-oz can of good Italian peeled plum tomatoes,
    drained and chopped
2 handfuls of black olives, pitted
salt and freshly ground black pepper
a splash of red wine vinegar (optional)
fresh stracci: 1 pasta recipe (page 98)
2 handfuls of fresh basil
2 handfuls of grated Parmesan cheese

In a large hot pan, fry the eggplant, coriander seeds and chillies in a couple of generous glugs of olive oil until they are nice and golden. Add more olive oil if needed. Add the chopped tomatoes and cook for 5 minutes before adding the olives. Continue cooking until you have a lovely "saucey" consistency. Season to taste at this point with salt, pepper and maybe a splash of red wine vinegar. Cook the stracci in salted boiling water until al dente. Drain and throw into the sauce. Toss, rip in the basil and serve with grated Parmesan on top.

# stracci with Gorgonzola, mascarpone, marjoram and walnuts

*serves 4*

1 clove of garlic, peeled and finely chopped

olive oil

2 good handfuls of marjoram, washed and picked from
    stems

5oz Gorgonzola cheese

9oz mascarpone cheese

fresh stracci: 1 pasta recipe (page 98)

7oz walnuts, shells removed

salt and freshly ground black pepper

1 good handful of grated Parmesan cheese

In a pan fry the garlic in a little olive oil with the marjoram until softened. Turn down the heat and add the Gorgonzola and mascarpone. Slowly melt the cheeses—don't let them boil. Cook your stracci in salted boiling water until al dente. Now turn up the heat under the cheese—again, don't let this boil—throwing in half the walnuts. Season to taste. Toss the drained stracci into the sauce, coat and serve sprinkled with the rest of the walnuts and the Parmesan.

# pappardelle

Cut the sheets of pasta to about the length of a shoebox. Fold them over twice, making sure you have dusted them generously on both sides with flour. Now cut into slices approximately 1½ inches wide (see picture on page 107) and you have your pappardelle. Remember to gently toss and jiggle the pappardelle around to separate the lengths of pasta once you have cut them. This will remove any excess flour.

## pappardelle with rabbit, herbs and cream

*serves 4*
2 good handfuls of fresh thyme, leaves picked from stems
salt and freshly ground black pepper
olive oil
rind of 2 lemons, peeled
4 legs of rabbit
1 clove of garlic, peeled and finely chopped
1 small red onion, peeled and finely chopped
3 good glasses of dry white wine
1⅓ cups of heavy cream
fresh pappardelle: 1 pasta recipe (page 98)
1 good handful of grated Parmesan cheese

Smash your thyme with a little pinch of salt and some pepper in a pestle and mortar and scrunch together with a couple of glugs of olive oil and the lemon rind. Massage this onto the legs of rabbit and set aside for 15 minutes to 1 hour. In a hot pan that you can put a tight-fitting lid on later, fry the rabbit until lightly golden. Then add the remaining marinade, garlic and onion and continue cooking until slightly softened. Add the white wine, place on the lid and simmer very slowly for about 1 hour, until tender. Continue checking to make sure that the liquid in the pan does not dry up (adding a little water if necessary). When the rabbit is cooked, allow to cool slightly, then use 2 forks to remove all the meat from the bones. Put the meat back into the pan with the cooking juices, add the cream and reheat. Cook your pappardelle in salted boiling water until al dente. Drain the pasta and toss with the creamy meat sauce. Remove from the heat, correct the seasoning and add the Parmesan, toss again and serve.

# pappardelle, spicy sausage meat and mixed wild mushrooms

You don't have to use your own freshly made pasta for this—you can get some really nice curly dried stuff, like the pasta seen here, which I nicked from my mate Gennaro.

*serves 4*
1 onion, peeled and finely chopped
1 clove of garlic, peeled and finely chopped
9oz of the best spicy sausages you can find, meat removed from skin
olive oil
2 good handfuls of fresh thyme, leaves picked from stems
1–2 small dried red chillies, crumbled, to taste
14oz mixed wild mushrooms (chanterelles, cepes or blewits, oyster and
    shiitake), torn
fresh pappardelle: 1 pasta recipe (page 98)
salt and freshly ground black pepper
3 very large pats of butter
1 handful of flat-leaf parsley, chopped
1 handful of grated Parmesan cheese

Fry the onion, garlic and sausage meat in a little olive oil until lightly golden. Add the thyme, chillies and mushrooms. Continue to fry, cooking away any moisture from the mushrooms. Cook the pappardelle in salted boiling water until al dente. Reserve a little cooking water. Remove the mushrooms from the heat, season to taste and loosen with the butter and a little cooking water from the pasta. Toss the drained pasta with the mushrooms and serve sprinkled with lots of parsley and some grated Parmesan.

# tagliatelle

Cut the sheets of pasta to about the length of a shoebox. Fold them over twice, making sure you have dusted them generously on both sides with flour. Now cut into slices around ½ inch wide (see picture on page 110) and you have your tagliatelle. Remember to gently toss and jiggle the tagliatelle around to separate the lengths of pasta once you have cut them. This will remove any excess flour.

## tagliatelle with saffron, seafood and cream

*serves 4*
a good pinch of saffron
1 glass of dry white wine
fresh tagliatelle: 1 pasta recipe (page 98)
olive oil
1 large clove of garlic, finely chopped
1½lb mixed seafood (red mullet, scallops,
   clams, bearded mussels, shrimp, squid)
1⅓ cups of heavy cream
salt and freshly ground black pepper
fennel tops, parsley or dill to garnish, chopped

Soak the saffron in the white wine. Cook the tagliatelle in salted boiling water until al dente. Add a little oil and the garlic to a frying pan and cook until softened. Add the clams and mussels, shake the pan around and add the white wine and saffron mixture. Bring to the boil, and discard any shellfish that remain closed. Then add the rest of the seafood and the cream. Simmer for 3–4 minutes, season to taste, add the drained tagliatelle and serve scattered with a few chopped fennel tops, parsley or dill.

# tagliatelle with tomato sauce, spinach and crumbled ricotta

*serves 4*

1 large clove of garlic, chopped
a pinch of dried chilli
olive oil
two 14-oz cans of whole plum tomatoes
red wine vinegar, to taste
salt and freshly ground black pepper
fresh tagliatelle: 1 pasta recipe (page 98)
9oz fresh spinach, washed
9oz fresh ricotta (preferably buffalo), seasoned and crumbled
extra-virgin olive oil

Fry the garlic and dried chilli in a little olive oil until softened. Add the tomatoes, bring to the boil, then reduce the heat to a simmer. The tomatoes should remain whole until they have cooked down into a thickish sauce. Break them up with a fork or spoon. Remove from the heat and season carefully to taste with a little red wine vinegar, salt, freshly ground black pepper and some good olive oil.

Cook the tagliatelle in salted boiling water until al dente. At the same time steam the spinach in a colander above the pasta. Drain the tagliatelle and stir into the tomato sauce. Serve with a generous amount of spinach on top and scattered with the ricotta. Finish with a drizzle of peppery extra-virgin olive oil.

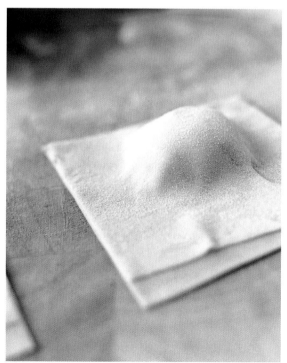

# making ravioli

After rolling out the pasta sheets to about 1mm thick and 4 inches wide (see page 104) you can fill them with your chosen filling to make ravioli. Work with 1 sheet at a time, covering the rest with a damp cloth.

*Stage 1*

Lay your pasta sheet on a generously flour-dusted surface with a good heaped teaspoon of filling in the middle of the sheet at one end. Repeat this all the way along the pasta at 2-inch intervals. Using a clean pastry brush dipped in a little water, lightly, evenly and thoroughly brush the pasta around the piles of filling. This will stick the pasta together. Place a second, similar-sized sheet of pasta on top of the first.

*Stage 2*

Working from one end of the pasta to the other, push the sheets together and around each mound of filling. Do this gently with the base of your palm, cupping and enclosing each filling in the pasta making sure you extract all the air.

*Stage 3*

Now cut the ravioli to shape with a knife or crinkly cutter wheel.

*Stage 4*

You can cook them straight away or keep them in the fridge on a flour-dusted tray for 3–4 hours if you want to eat them later.

# ravioli of minted asparagus with potatoes and mascarpone

*serves 4–6*

8oz potatoes, peeled

1¹⁄₂lb asparagus, bases trimmed and stalks peeled
   (if need be)

1 clove of garlic, finely chopped

olive oil

salt and freshly ground black pepper

1 good handful of fresh mint, leaves picked from stems and
   chopped

1 fresh pasta recipe (page 98)

2 very large pats of butter

2 heaped tablespoons mascarpone cheese, lightly seasoned
   with salt and pepper

1 handful of grated Parmesan cheese


Cook the potatoes in salted boiling water until tender, then drain. Remove the tips of the asparagus and set to one side. Finely slice the stalks and fry with the garlic in a little olive oil until tender, placing a lid on the pan. Remove from the heat, add the potatoes and mash together. Season carefully and add half the chopped mint to taste. Fill your ravioli with a heaped teaspoon of filling (page 113) and cook in salted boiling water with the asparagus tips for 3–4 minutes. Drain and toss the ravioli and asparagus tips with the butter, mascarpone, Parmesan and the rest of the mint.

# ravioli of creamed ricotta, toasted pine nuts, Parmesan and loadsa herbs

*serves 4–6*

14oz ricotta cheese

1 large egg yolk

2 good handfuls of grated Parmesan cheese

2 handfuls of pine nuts, toasted and crushed

3 large handfuls of mixed herbs (green and purple basil, parsley),
    roughly chopped

salt and freshly ground black pepper

a pinch of nutmeg

1 fresh pasta recipe (page 98)

extra-virgin olive oil

With a fork, beat the ricotta, egg yolk and most of the Parmesan together until light and creamy. Stir in your pine nuts and herbs and season carefully with salt, pepper and nutmeg. Fill your ravioli with a good teaspoon of filling (page 113) and cook in salted boiling water for 3–4 minutes. Serve drizzled with extra-virgin olive oil and the remaining Parmesan.

# making tortellini

After rolling out the pasta sheets to about 1mm thick and 4 inches wide (see page 98) you can fill them with your chosen filling to make tortellini. Work with 1 sheet at a time, covering the rest with a damp cloth.

*Stage 1*

Lay a sheet of pasta out on a flour-dusted surface. Cut into 4 × 4 inch squares. On each square, place a good teaspoon of filling just off-center. With a clean pastry brush evenly brush a little water around each mound of filling. Do this thoroughly to guarantee a good seal.

*Stage 2*

Fold each square in half from corner to corner, enclosing the filling—don't worry if they look a bit uneven, as we want them to look homemade. Tightly seal the tortellini together by cupping your hand around each mound of filling and pressing down. Make sure all the air is extracted.

*Stage 3*

With the flat edge of each tortellini facing you, roll them once toward the tip.

*Stage 4*

Bring the two side flaps into the center and squeeze them together tightly where they meet. You can cook them straight away or keep them in the fridge on a flour-dusted tray for 3–4 hours if you want to eat them later.

# tortellini of ricotta, lemon, Parmesan and sage butter

*serves 4–6*
14oz ricotta cheese, preferably buffalo
zest and juice of 2 lemons
1 good handful of grated pecorino cheese
1 good handful of grated Parmesan cheese
salt and freshly ground black pepper
1 fresh pasta recipe (page 98)
2 very large pats of butter
1 good handful of sage, leaves picked from stems

With a fork mix together the ricotta, lemon zest, pecorino and most of the Parmesan, and season carefully. Fill your tortellini with a teaspoon of filling (page 113) and cook in salted boiling water for 3–4 minutes. Heat a large frying pan, add the butter and sage and cook until the sage is crisp and the butter is foaming but not coloring. Throw in your drained tortellini and squeeze in some of the lemon juice to taste. Serve immediately and sprinkle generously with the remaining Parmesan.

## I-Thai-fried tortellini of chicken, ginger, water chestnut and lemongrass with dipping sauce

This is a bastardization of the fantastic *gyozas* (Japanese dumplings) served at Wagamama bistros in London. They can even be deep fried for a really mad crispy texture. It's fine to improvise, using shrimp, pork or vegetables in the filling.

*serves 6*
a couple of thumb-sized pieces of fresh ginger, peeled
2 cloves of garlic, peeled
3 stalks of lemongrass, outer leaves removed, chopped
4 legs of chicken, preferably organic, bone removed
2 good handfuls of fresh cilantro, including stalks
2 tablespoons sesame seed oil
1 large egg
2 level tablespoons cornstarch
2 handfuls of canned water chestnuts
salt and freshly ground black pepper
1 fresh pasta recipe (page 98)
olive oil

In a food processor finely whizz up your ginger, garlic and lemongrass. Add your chicken meat and whizz for a further minute. Add the rest of the ingredients except the pasta and olive oil and pulse the food processor until you achieve an interesting, smoothish texture. Start to fill your tortellini with a teaspoon of filling (page 113). Once they are filled, cook them for 3–4 minutes in salted boiling water. Remove, drain and place the tortellini into a hot nonstick pan drizzled with a couple of glugs of olive oil. Fry until one side is crisp and golden, then remove straight away and serve with the dipping sauce.

## tasty dipping sauce

You can vary this dipping sauce to your own preference, using things like kaffir lime leaves, lime juice and ginger as possibilities.

³/₄ cup soy sauce
4 tablespoons rice wine or white wine vinegar
2 teaspoons sugar
½ fresh chilli, finely chopped
a little fresh cilantro, chopped

Put all the ingredients into a bowl and stir. Divide into little dipping bowls to serve.

# dried pasta

A lot of people think that fresh pasta is superior to dried—that's rubbish, it's just that they do different things. Dried pasta is generally made from flour and mostly water, which means that it lasts for ages and retains a fantastic bite which is great for seafood, oily and tomato sauces, whereas fresh pasta is silky and tender and suits being stuffed and served with creamy and buttery sauces. Here are some of my favorite dried pasta recipes.

## spaghetti with squashed olives, tomatoes, garlic, olive oil and chopped arugula

*serves 4*
olive oil
1 clove of garlic, finely chopped
1 small dried chilli, to taste
3 good handfuls of cherry or plum tomatoes,
   seeded and roughly chopped
1 good handful of olives, crushed and pitted
1lb dried spaghetti, the best you can get
salt and freshly ground black pepper
3 good handfuls of arugula, roughly chopped

Heat up a large frying pan, add a couple of good glugs of olive oil and fry the garlic and chilli for 30 seconds before adding the tomatoes and olives. Toss and allow to cook for a further 4–6 minutes. Meanwhile, cook your spaghetti in salted boiling water until al dente. The tomatoes will thicken into a lovely sauce with some nice fresh chunks in it as well. Toss and add to your drained pasta. Season to taste.

Add the chopped arugula, toss quickly, and serve in a big bowl immediately. Don't waste any time—get it on the table, let people help themselves and have a nice big green salad, a bit of bread and some wine. Lovely, fantastic.

## spaghetti with olive oil, garlic, chilli and parsley

*serves 4*
1lb dried spaghetti, the best you can get
1 large clove of garlic, finely chopped
olive oil
1–2 fresh red chillies, seeded and finely chopped
1 good handful of flat-leaf parsley, finely chopped
salt and freshly ground black pepper

While cooking the spaghetti in salted boiling water until al dente, fry the garlic in a couple of good glugs of olive oil until softened. Add your chillies, drained pasta and parsley. Toss to coat, season and serve.

## spaghetti with red onions, sun-dried tomatoes, balsamic vinegar and basil

*serves 4*
1lb dried spaghetti, the best you can get
1 red onion, peeled and finely chopped
olive oil
2 handfuls of sun-dried tomatoes in oil, chopped
3 tablespoons balsamic vinegar
salt and freshly ground black pepper
2 handfuls of basil, torn
1 small handful of Parmesan or pecorino cheese, grated

While cooking the spaghetti in salted boiling water until al dente, slowly fry the onion in a couple of glugs of olive oil for 5 minutes until soft and tender. Stir in the tomatoes and vinegar, and throw in your drained pasta. Season and toss together with the basil. Serve with grated Parmesan or pecorino.

# spaghetti with anchovies, dried chilli and pangritata

Pangritata is great. It's basically bread crumbs fried or toasted in garlic oil. In Italy, pangritata was once used as a substitute for Parmesan, which some people couldn't afford. It gives a dish an excellent texture and crunch and, if made well, great flavor.

*serves 4*
*for the pangritata*
1/2 cup olive oil
1 clove of garlic, sliced
1 good handful of fresh thyme, leaves picked from stems
7oz fresh bread crumbs
salt and freshly ground black pepper

1lb dried spaghetti, the best you can get
6 tablespoons extra-virgin olive oil
2 cloves of garlic, finely chopped
16 anchovy fillets
juice of 2 lemons
2 small dried red chillies, crumbled

First make the pangritata. Put the olive oil into a hot thick-bottomed pan. Add the garlic, thyme and bread crumbs; they will fry and begin to toast. Stir for a couple of minutes until the bread crumbs are really crisp and golden. Season with a little salt and freshly ground black pepper and drain on paper towels.

Cook the spaghetti in salted boiling water until al dente. While it is cooking, put the oil and garlic in a pan and heat gently. As the garlic begins to soften, lay the anchovy fillets over the top. After a minute you will see them begin to melt. Squeeze in the lemon juice and sprinkle in the dried chillies. Toss in the drained spaghetti and coat it in the sauce. Taste a bit of pasta—it may need a little more lemon juice and a little extra seasoning. Serve straight away, sprinkled really generously with the pangritata.

# linguine with pancetta, olive oil, chilli, clams and white wine

*serves 4*

1lb dried linguine, the best you can get

olive oil

4 strips of pancetta or lean bacon, sliced thinly

1 large clove of garlic, finely chopped

1–2 dried red chillies, crumbled

1½ lb littleneck or Manila clams

2 glasses of dry white wine

1 good handful of flat-leaf parsley, roughly chopped

salt and freshly ground black pepper

Cook your linguine in salted boiling water until al dente. Meanwhile, get a pan hot and add a couple of good glugs of olive oil and the pancetta. Fry until golden, then add the garlic and chillies. Let soften slightly and add the clams. Stir, then add the white wine. Put a lid on the pan and cook for a further couple of minutes until all the clams have opened—discard any that remain closed. Remove from the heat and add the drained linguine. Stir in the parsley, correct the seasoning and serve with all the cooking juices.

# linguine puttanesca

*serves 4*

1lb dried linguine, the best you can get

3 cloves of garlic, finely chopped

2–3 small dried red chillies, crumbled

1 teaspoon dried oregano

extra-virgin olive oil

two 14-oz cans of tomatoes, drained and chopped

2 handfuls of big black olives, pitted

1 handful of capers, soaked in water and drained

12 anchovy fillets, roughly chopped

1 good handful of fresh basil

salt and freshly ground black pepper

Cook your linguine in salted boiling water until al dente. Meanwhile fry the garlic, chillies and oregano in a little olive oil until slightly softened. Add the tomatoes and bring to a simmer. Add the olives, capers and anchovies and continue to cook for about another 4 or 5 minutes, until you have a lovely tomato sauce consistency. Remove from the heat, plunge the drained linguine into it, toss it and cover with the sauce. Rip and scatter the basil over the pasta, correct the seasoning and drizzle with good extra-virgin olive oil.

# farfalle with broccoli, anchovies and chilli

*serves 4*
2 heads of broccoli
1 large clove of garlic, finely chopped
15 anchovy fillets
2–3 small dried red chillies, crumbled
olive oil
1lb dried farfalle, the best you can get
salt and freshly ground black pepper
1 handful of pine nuts, lightly toasted

Remove the florets from the broccoli and trim, peel and finely chop the stalks. In a pan fry the garlic, anchovies, chillies and all the broccoli, stalks and florets, very slowly in a couple of glugs of olive oil for about 15 minutes with the lid on, adding a little water if need be. Feel free to mash some of the broccoli up as it cooks, giving you a chunky puréed sauce. Season to taste. Cook your farfalle in salted boiling water until al dente. Mix the drained pasta with your tasty sauce, adding a little cooking liquid to thin if necessary, throwing in the pine nuts just before serving.

# farfalle with Savoy cabbage, pancetta, thyme and mozzarella

*serves 4*

10 strips of pancetta or lean bacon, thinly sliced
olive oil
1 clove of garlic, finely chopped
1 good handful of thyme, leaves picked from stems
1 large Savoy cabbage (outer leaves removed),
    quartered, cored and finely sliced
1 handful of grated Parmesan cheese
1lb dried farfalle, the best you can get
salt and freshly ground black pepper
extra-virgin olive oil
7oz buffalo mozzarella, cut into ½-inch dice
2 handfuls of pine nuts, lightly toasted

In a pan fry your pancetta in a little olive oil until lightly golden. Add the garlic and thyme and cook until softened. Add the Savoy cabbage and Parmesan, then stir and put the lid on the pan. Cook for a further 5 minutes, shaking every now and again, while you cook your farfalle in salted boiling water until al dente. When the cabbage is nice and tender, season and loosen with some nice peppery extra-virgin olive oil. Toss the drained farfalle into the cabbage mixture and at the last minute mix in the mozzarella and pine nuts. Serve immediately.

# return of the risotto

I think this is the best basic risotto recipe you will come across—you will find it really easy. I assure you that once you've got the knack you'll carry on making it all the time and it won't let you down. You can so easily enhance it by adding different seasonal ingredients. So here's the basic risotto, which will give you an amazingly creamy base, followed by some simple recipes to take the dish in completely different directions.

*serves 6*

approximately 5 cups stock (chicken, fish or vegetable
   as appropriate—pages 275–6)
1 tablespoon olive oil
3 shallots or 2 medium onions, finely chopped
2 cloves of garlic, finely chopped
1/2 a head of celery, finely chopped
14oz medium-grain rice, such as arborio
2 wineglasses of dry white vermouth (dry Martini or
   Noilly Prat) or dry white wine
sea salt and freshly ground black pepper
5 tablespoons butter
4oz freshly grated Parmesan cheese

*Stage 1*

Heat the stock. In a separate pan heat the olive oil, add the shallots or onions, garlic and celery, and fry slowly for about 4 minutes. When the vegetables have softened, add the rice and turn up the heat.

*Stage 2*

The rice will now begin to fry, so keep stirring it. After a minute it will look slightly translucent. Add the vermouth or wine and keep stirring—it will smell fantastic. Any harsh alcohol flavors will evaporate and leave the rice with a tasty essence.

*Stage 3*

Once the vermouth or wine has cooked into the rice, add your first ladle of hot stock and a good pinch of salt. Turn down the heat to a highish simmer so the rice doesn't cook too quickly on the outside. Keep adding ladlefuls of stock, stirring and almost massaging the creamy starch from the rice, allowing each ladleful to be absorbed before adding the next. This will take around 15 minutes. Taste the rice—is it cooked?

Carry on adding stock until the rice is soft but with a slight *bite*. Don't forget to check the seasoning carefully.

*Stage 4*

Remove from the heat and add the butter and Parmesan. Stir gently. Place a lid on the pan and allow to sit for 2–3 minutes. This is the most important part of making the risotto, as this is when it becomes outrageously creamy and oozy like it should be. Eat as soon as possible while the risotto retains its perfect texture.

## roasted sweet garlic, thyme and mascarpone risotto with toasted almonds and bread crumbs

Don't be scared by this one—the garlic is not overpowering, it's an extremely subtle and delicate combination.

*serves 6*
2 large heads of garlic, whole and unpeeled
1 basic risotto recipe (pages 134–5)
1 good handful of fresh thyme, leaves picked from stems
5$\frac{1}{2}$oz shelled and peeled almonds, lightly crushed, cracked
   or chopped
2 handfuls of coarse fresh bread crumbs
olive oil
salt
2 heaped tablespoons mascarpone cheese

Roast the whole garlic heads on a dish in a 450°F oven for about 30 minutes until soft. Separate the cloves and squeeze out the sweet insides. Add with the thyme at the start of Stage 3 of the basic risotto recipe. In a frying pan toast the almonds and bread crumbs in a little olive oil until crisp and golden. Season with a little salt. Set to one side. Serve the risotto with a dollop of mascarpone on the top and sprinkled with the toasted almonds and bread crumbs. Lovely.

## white risotto with lemon thyme, sliced prosciutto, pecorino and crumbled goat's cheese

I initially made this risotto pretty much off the cuff with leftover cheese from my fridge and a snip of lemon thyme from my windowbox. It was perfect. Use ordinary thyme if you cannot get hold of lemon thyme.

*serves 6*
1 basic risotto recipe (pages 134–5)
2 good handfuls of fresh lemon thyme, leaves picked from
    stems
4oz pecorino cheese, grated
8 slices prosciutto
5½oz goat's cheese, crumbled

At the start of Stage 3 of the basic risotto recipe add the lemon thyme. When you stir in your butter and Parmesan at Stage 4, add the pecorino. Lay the prosciutto slices over the risotto just before eating and serve with the goat's cheese crumbled over the top. Scatter with a little extra thyme leaves if you like.

# shrimp and pea risotto with basil and mint

For me this risotto really works because of the natural sweetness you get in peas and shrimp. With a little help from some delicate herbs it will put a smile on your face. Remember not to use any Parmesan in your basic risotto recipe—not good with fish. If using fresh peas, add the pods to the stock to give it a good pea flavor rather than throwing them away. Results with good frozen peas are also brilliant.

*serves 6*
1 basic risotto recipe (pages 134–5)
3 good handfuls of fresh peas, shelled
1 large pat of butter
a little stock
1lb raw shrimp, uncooked, shelled
1 handful of fresh basil, chopped
$1/2$ handful of fresh mint, chopped
juice of 1 lemon
extra-virgin olive oil

Fry half the peas in the butter and a little of the stock from the basic recipe. Cook until tender and mash. Add this at the end of Stage 3 of the basic risotto recipe with the shrimp and the rest of the peas and simmer for 2 minutes—shrimp and peas take no time to cook. At Stage 4 throw in the fresh herbs and squeeze in the lemon juice. Stir and serve immediately. Drizzle with really nice peppery extra-virgin olive oil.

# risotto of radicchio, bacon, rosemary and red wine

*serves 6*
1 basic risotto recipe (pages 134–5)
3 wineglasses of your favorite full-bodied red wine
10 strips bacon, finely sliced
olive oil
2 heads of radicchio, trimmed and finely sliced
1 handful of fresh rosemary
1 pat of butter

Add the red wine in place of the vermouth or white wine at Stage 2 of the basic risotto recipe. Fry your bacon in a little olive oil until slightly golden. Add the radicchio and rosemary to the pan with the butter and cook gently with the lid on until wilted. At the start of Stage 3 stir in the bacon, radicchio and rosemary.

joe

fish and shellfish

# monkfish wrapped in banana leaves with ginger, cilantro, chilli and coconut milk

You just can't go wrong with this combination of flavors. It's open to all white fish, especially swordfish, cod, haddock and monkfish. Banana leaves are very easy to buy from Asian stores. Get nice big ones to wrap your fish up in. Failing banana leaves, you can use grapevine leaves, which you can get in the supermarket—somewhat smaller, but no less tasty for that. If you really can't get hold of any leaves, then aluminum foil will do.

*serves 4*
4 large banana leaves or grapevine leaves
a little olive oil
2 fresh chillies, red, green or both
2 stalks of lemongrass, outer leaves removed, finely chopped
1 clove of garlic, finely chopped
2 good handfuls of fresh cilantro, roughly chopped
juice and zest of 2 limes
2 tablespoons sesame seed oil
2 heaped tablespoons finely sliced fresh ginger
6–8oz monkfish per person
one 14-oz can of coconut milk
4 rosemary sprigs or bay leaf stalks, to secure

Preheat the oven to 450°F. Lay out your banana leaves and rub them with olive oil. Leaving aside your fish, coconut milk and the rosemary sprigs or bay leaf stalks, sprinkle a little bit of everything else on one end of each leaf. Place your fish on top and then sprinkle what's left over them. Pour 5–6 tablespoons of coconut milk into each parcel before folding the leaf over the fish, bringing the sides in and spiking it with a rosemary sprig or bay leaf stalk to secure it. This will look lovely and it's natural, but I have been known to use a clothespin or string to hold it all together. It won't be a perfect seal but this allows it to breathe and steam, letting the flavors infuse. So gutsy and tasty. Put your parcels on a tray and bake for 15 minutes, then remove from the oven and allow to rest for 5 minutes.

I serve the individual parcels on plates at the table and let my friends dissect them. When opened, the fragrant steam wafts up and smells fantastic. Serve with plain boiled rice to mop up the juices—that's all it has to be. End of story, done, lovely.

# baked cod with French beans, pancetta and pine nuts

Another superb combination. The French beans, pancetta and pine nuts go amazingly well together. It's a great way to cook the cod because it's all in one pan, which means hardly any washing up.

*serves 4*
1½lb French beans, trimmed and sliced at an angle
1 clove of garlic, finely sliced
salt and freshly ground black pepper
olive oil
four 8-oz cod steaks, on the bone
12 strips of smoked pancetta or bacon
1 good handful of pine nuts
2 lemons, halved

Preheat the oven to 425°F. Place your French beans in an appropriately sized roasting pan. Throw in your garlic and a little salt and pepper, add just enough olive oil to coat the beans, and mix it all around. Nestle the cod steaks in among the beans, lightly season again, and then place some pancetta over the cod and among the beans. Sprinkle with pine nuts and drizzle a little olive oil over the top. Take your lemon halves and place them in the pan—they will cook and color slightly, going jammy, sweet and lemony. Fantastic.

Cook for roughly 15 minutes in the middle of the preheated oven. Lightly lay aluminum foil over the fish for the first 5 minutes and then remove it. You know the cod is cooked when the bone in the middle is easily removed. This is a meal in itself, so serve with all the lovely juices from the pan drizzled over the top.

# whole sea bass baked in a bag and stuffed with herbs

This is a great way to cook fish, letting it retain all its natural juices and moisture and rewarding you with the most fantastic tasty sauce. I think the fish is best served in its bag in the middle of the table—it's real theater. When the bag is broken open the fragrant smells waft all around the table, leaving everyone salivating for it.

*serves 4*

one 4-lb sea bass or two 2-lb sea bass, scaled and gutted

1 red onion, peeled and finely sliced

1 bulb of fennel, finely sliced

1 clove of garlic, peeled and finely chopped

sea salt and freshly ground black pepper

1 tablespoon fennel seeds

4 handfuls of mixed fresh herbs
 (parsley, basil, fennel, dill, tarragon, marjoram, bay)

3 lemons

6 good glugs of extra-virgin olive oil

Preheat the oven to 425°F. Tear off a piece of aluminum foil 5 times as long as your fish, then fold this in half to give you double thickness. In the middle of one half of the foil sprinkle the red onion, fennel and garlic. Place your fish snugly on top of the veg. Season the inside and outside of the fish with sea salt, freshly ground black pepper and the fennel seeds, then stuff with all your herbs—use just one herb or a mixture of your favorites. Squeeze over the juice of 2 of the lemons, slice the third lemon and tuck it around the fish, and pour over the olive oil.

Fold the foil over the fish and seal the three edges neatly and tightly, being careful not to pierce the foil as this will let the juices escape. Set on a baking sheet and cook in the preheated oven for 10 minutes per 1lb. If using a 4-lb fish, then obviously give it 40 minutes, if using 2 two-pounders then you only need to cook them for 20 minutes. Once removed from the oven, allow the fish to rest for 5 minutes before serving at the table. Nice with simple boiled potatoes and a crisp salad.

# wok-cooked fragrant mussels

I had the idea for this dish while eating mussels in New York. It takes literally minutes to cook and tastes absolutely pukka. Simply serve with plain boiled or steamed rice.

*serves 4–6*
4¹/₂lb best live mussels, debearded
olive oil
2 cloves of garlic, finely sliced
3 stalks of lemongrass, outer leaves removed, finely sliced
2 fresh chillies, red, green or both
3 tablespoons finely sliced fresh ginger
2 handfuls of fresh cilantro, pounded or finely chopped
1 tablespoon sesame seed oil
salt and freshly ground black pepper
5 scallions, finely sliced
juice of 3 limes
one 14-oz can of coconut milk

Place your mussels with a couple of glugs of olive oil in a large, very hot wok or pot. Shake and add the rest of the ingredients, apart from the lime juice and coconut milk. Keep turning over until all the mussels have opened—throw away any that remain closed. Squeeze in your lime juice and add your coconut milk. Bring to the boil and serve immediately.

## roasted slashed fillet of sea bass stuffed with herbs, baked on mushroom potatoes with salsa verde—à la Tony Blair

I cooked this for British Prime Minister Tony Blair and the Italian prime minister at the British/Italian summit a few years ago. It went down a treat so I thought I'd put it in the book. This is a really great way to cook sea bass. Try to get the fattest bass fillets you can find. Failing that, red snapper or hake are fantastic cooked this way too.

*serves 4*
four 8-oz sea bass fillets
1 handful of mixed herbs (green or purple basil, flat-leaf
    parsley, thyme), roughly chopped
2¼lb potatoes, scrubbed
olive oil
2 cloves of garlic, finely chopped
salt and freshly ground black pepper
3 large pats of butter
1lb mixed, preferably wild, mushrooms, torn or roughly
    chopped
3 lemons
1 salsa verde recipe (page 277)

Preheat the oven to 475°F. Put a bit of wax paper on the bottom of a shallow baking pan, rubbed with olive oil. Slash the fish fillets about halfway down and stuff the slashes with the herbs. Slice the potatoes lengthwise, just under ½ inch thick. Dry them off with paper towels and very lightly coat them with olive oil. Mix in half of your garlic, season with salt and pepper, then lay them in one layer on the pan. Cook the potatoes in the oven for around 15 minutes, until just cooked. Remove and put to one side.

Put the rest of the garlic into a pan with 2 pats of butter and a glug of olive oil. Fry your mixed mushrooms and season until tasty. If water comes out of them just continue cooking until it evaporates. Take the pan off the heat, squeeze in the juice from 1 lemon and stir in the remaining butter. Now scatter the mushrooms over the potatoes and kind of rub them in on top, underneath, all over. Place your sea bass fillets on top. Now bake in the oven for 12–15 minutes, depending on the thickness of your fish.

Remove the tray from the oven, put some aluminum foil over the top and let it sit for about 5 minutes, during which time all the lovely juices will run out into the potatoes. Serve it with salsa verde, half a lemon each and a glass of crisp white wine.

# fantastic fish pie

The whole fish pie thing is one of the most homely and comforting dinners I can think of. This is a cracking recipe which does it for me.

*serves 6*
5 large potatoes, peeled and diced into 1-inch squares
salt and freshly ground black pepper
2 large eggs
2 large handfuls of fresh spinach
1 onion, finely chopped
1 carrot, halved and finely chopped
extra-virgin olive oil
approximately 1⅓ cups heavy cream
2 good handfuls of grated sharp Cheddar or Parmesan cheese
juice of 1 lemon
1 heaped teaspoon English mustard
1 large handful of flat-leaf parsley, finely chopped
1lb haddock or cod fillet, skin removed,
   pin-boned and sliced into strips
fresh nutmeg (optional)

Preheat the oven to 450°F. Put the potatoes into salted boiling water and bring back to a boil for 2 minutes. Carefully add the eggs to the pan and cook for a further 8 minutes, until hard-boiled, by which time the potatoes should also be cooked. At the same time, steam the spinach in a colander above the pan. This will take only a minute. When the spinach is done, remove from the colander and gently squeeze out any excess moisture. Then drain the potatoes in the colander. Remove the eggs, cool under cold water, then peel and quarter them. Place to one side.

In a separate pan slowly fry the onion and carrot in a little olive oil for about 5 minutes, then add the cream and bring just to the boil. Remove from the heat and add the cheese, lemon juice, mustard and parsley. Put the spinach, fish and eggs into an appropriately sized earthenware dish and mix together, pouring over the creamy vegetable sauce. The cooked potatoes should be drained and mashed—add a bit of olive oil, salt, pepper and a touch of grated nutmeg if you like. Spread on top of the fish. Don't bother piping it to make it look pretty—it's a homely hearty thing. Place in the oven for about 25–30 minutes until the potatoes are golden. Serve with some nice peas or greens, not forgetting your baked beans and ketchup. Tacky but tasty and that's what I like.

## seared scallops and crispy prosciutto with roasted tomatoes and smashed white beans

*serves 4*

4 large ripe plum tomatoes, quartered
salt and freshly ground black pepper
a pinch of dried oregano
olive oil
8 slices of prosciutto
1 small clove of garlic, finely chopped
1–2 small dried red chillies, crumbled, to taste
4–6 anchovy fillets, chopped
one 14-oz can of cannellini beans or flageolet beans, drained
extra-virgin olive oil
12–16 scallops, trimmed with roe on or off to your preference
1 olive oil and lemon juice dressing (page 81)
a small handful of peppery greens (arugula or watercress)

Preheat the oven to 475°F. Season the tomatoes and sprinkle with the oregano. Drizzle with olive oil and roast in the oven skin side down for about 10–15 minutes. Place the prosciutto slices beside the tomatoes and continue to roast for a further 10 minutes, until the tomatoes are juicy and the prosciutto is crisp. In a pan fry the garlic, chillies and anchovies in a glug of olive oil for a minute or so. Add your beans and cook for a couple of minutes before adding a wineglass of water. Bring to the boil, then lightly mash to a coarse purée. Loosen the purée with a little more water if need be. Finish the flavor off with some peppery extra-virgin olive oil, salt and freshly ground black pepper.

Season the scallops, then sear them in a frying pan with a touch of olive oil for 2 minutes without touching them. Check and continue to fry until they have a lovely sweet caramelized skin—turn them over and allow the other side to do the same. Don't overcook them. Remove to a bowl and coat with a little olive oil and lemon juice dressing. Put some smashed bean purée on each plate, scatter over the tomatoes, prosciutto and scallops, and finish off with some peppery greens.

# baked trout and potatoes with a crème fraîche, walnut and horseradish sauce

Trout is a fantastic and readily available fish. The combination of hot horseradish, nutty walnuts and creamy crème fraîche is a pukka marriage with trout as well as with the more obvious beef and lamb.

*serves 4*
1lb potatoes, peeled and finely sliced
olive oil
salt and freshly ground black pepper
4 whole trout, approximately 14oz–1lb each,
    gutted and scaled
1 heaped tablespoon grated fresh horseradish
9oz crème fraîche (about 1 generous cup)
2 handfuls of fresh walnuts, shelled and crushed
juice of 1 lemon

*optional*
a little fresh thyme, leaves picked from stems
1 lemon, sliced

Preheat the oven to 475°F. Dry your sliced potatoes with paper towels and lightly coat with olive oil. Season and place in a single layer in a large roasting pan. Place on a low oven shelf and roast for around 15 minutes, until crisp and golden. Meanwhile pat the trout dry, then with a sharp knife slash each fish at an angle on both sides—this will allow the heat and seasoning to penetrate. Rub with olive oil and seasoning. For extra flavor you can stuff the fish with fragrant herbs. I like to use thyme with some lemon slices too. The fish should only take a couple of minutes to prepare. Cook for around 12 minutes at the top of the oven until crisp and golden.

While the fish and potatoes are cooking make your sauce. Fresh horseradish, which you should peel and grate, is nicer, but you can also use the creamed horseradish bought in jars. Not quite as hot but still tasty. Mix the horseradish in a bowl with the crème fraîche and the walnuts and season well. Squeeze over some lemon juice to taste.

Serve the fish and potatoes side by side with a good lob of the crème fraîche sauce. Really nice with a green salad, some buttered bread and a glass of beer.

## grilled swordfish, green beans and spicy tomato salsa

*serves 4*
four 6–8-oz swordfish steaks (1/2 inch thick)
olive oil
salt and freshly ground black pepper
2 handfuls of green beans, cooked until tender
5 handfuls of mixed salad greens (watercress, arugula,
    radicchio, dandelion)
1 olive oil and lemon juice dressing (page 81)
1 tomato salsa recipe (page 277)

Rub the swordfish steaks with a little bit of olive oil, salt and freshly ground black pepper. Place on a very hot ridged griddle pan or grill and char for 2 minutes on each side. Remove from the pan. Lightly dress the beans and salad greens with the olive oil and lemon juice dressing. Rip up the swordfish and place it in and among the beans and salad leaves. Smear over the spicy tomato salsa before serving.

# wok-fried crispy sunfish with steamed Chinese greens and Thai dressing

*serves 2*

two 10–14-oz sunfish (or use sole or grouper)

2 Asian marinade recipes (page 194)

sunflower oil

flour, for dusting

2 good handfuls of Chinese greens
  (spinach, choi sum, bok choi, Chinese broccoli)

1 Thai dressing recipe (page 80)

Slash the sunfish on both sides, about ¹/₂ inch deep, in a crisscross fashion. In a pestle and mortar pound up the marinade then rub it into the fish, getting it into the cuts and the belly. Let this sit for up to an hour at cool room temperature or in the refrigerator.

Heat a wok with about 2–3 inches of sunflower oil in it. Put a bit of potato into the oil and when it is nicely golden you know the wok is hot enough—be very careful with the hot oil. Remove the sunfish from the marinade and pat dry with paper towels. Dust each fish with flour, shaking off any excess. Then carefully place each fish into the wok and fry for 3 minutes on each side. The skin will go amazingly crispy. Steam the greens in a colander above boiling water until tender. To serve, place the greens on a plate, put the fish on top, and smear and drizzle with the Thai dressing.

# salmon fillet wrapped in prosciutto with herby lentils, spinach and yogurt

*serves 4*
9oz lentils
four 8oz salmon fillets, skinned and pin-boned
salt and freshly ground black pepper
8 slices of prosciutto
olive oil
juice of 1 lemon
2 good handfuls of mixed herbs (flat-leaf parsley, basil, mint), chopped
3 large handfuls of spinach, chopped
$^3/_4$ cup plain yogurt

Preheat the oven to 425°F. Put the lentils into a pan, cover with water, bring to a boil and simmer until tender. Season the salmon fillets with a little pepper before wrapping them in the prosciutto slices. Leave some of the flesh exposed. Drizzle with olive oil and roast in the oven for around 10 minutes until the prosciutto is golden. Feel free to cook the salmon for less time if pinker is to your liking. Drain away most of the water from the lentils and season carefully with salt, pepper, the lemon juice and 4 good glugs of olive oil. Just before serving, stir the herbs and spinach into the lentils over high heat, until wilted. Place onto plates with the salmon and finish with a drizzle of yogurt seasoned lightly with salt and pepper and stirred well. Thin the yogurt with a little milk if necessary.

meat,
poultry
and game

# roast loin of pork with peaches

Pork, peaches, butter and thyme is one of the most luscious combinations I've ever had. You must try it.

*serves 6*
one 7-rib loin of pork, preferably organic
1 bunch of fresh thyme, leaves picked from stems and chopped
¾ cup plus 2 tablespoons butter
salt and freshly ground black pepper
8 fresh peaches (or use 2 16-oz cans in natural juice), halved and
   pitted

Preheat the oven to 425°F. Score the skin of your pork about ½ inch apart through the fat nearly to the meat. With a knife carefully part the meat from the ribs. Scrunch your chopped thyme into the butter with the seasoning. Rub and distribute a little of the butter into the gap you have made between the ribs and the meat. Push in as many peaches as you can fit and pack the rest of the butter on top. To hug the meat and ribs together and hold the peaches in place, simply fasten some string around the pork loin in 3 or 4 places and tie firmly. Place in a roasting pan with any leftover peaches and other veg you wish to cook with it—potatoes, parsnips, celeriac and Jerusalem artichokes are all good—and cook for 50 minutes to 1 hour, allowing it to rest for 10 minutes before serving. I usually make a little bit of homemade gravy in the roasting pan after removing the pork and veg. The sticky, sweet goodness is great when boiled with a little water or wine and any extra juices from the pork. Tasty.

# braised five-hour lamb with wine, veg and all that

This is a real hearty and trouble-free dinner. There's barely any preparation, just a nice long cooking time that will reward you with the most tender meat and tasty sauce. Large legs of lamb are ideal for this dish, as they benefit from slow cooking. If using a smaller leg of spring lamb, then consider cooking for an hour less.

*serves 6*
1 large leg of lamb
salt and freshly ground black pepper
olive oil
6 strips of bacon
3 red onions, peeled and quartered
3 cloves of garlic, peeled and sliced
2 good handfuls of mixed fresh herbs (thyme, rosemary, bay)
4 large potatoes, peeled and cut into chunks
1 celeriac, peeled and cut into chunks
6 large carrots, scrubbed and halved
3 parsnips, scrubbed and halved
one 750-ml bottle of dry white wine

Preheat the oven to 325°F. In a large casserole pot or a deep roasting pan, fry your well-seasoned lamb in a couple of good glugs of olive oil until brown on all sides. Add the bacon, onions and garlic and continue to fry for 3 more minutes. Throw in your herbs and veg, pour in your wine plus an equivalent amount of water, bring to the boil, and tightly cover with aluminum foil. Bake in the preheated oven for 5 hours, until tender, seasoning the cooking liquid to taste. To serve, pull away a nice portion of meat, take a selection of veg and serve with some crusty bread to mop up the gravy.

# seared encrusted carpaccio of beef

The reason I like to make this dish is because, apart from being really quick and simple, it's a sociable feast where everyone can tuck in and help themselves. I love all that. I always serve this on a large plate in the middle of the table, with crusty bread and a glass of wine. Any leftovers are even more gorgeous the next day.

A good carpaccio is always made from a prime cut of meat or fish, like loin or fillet, and it is normally served completely rare. To make it different I sear it lightly, encrusting a fantastic flavor on the outside but still leaving it delicately and classically raw.

Here I will show you how to sear a fillet of beef with a tasty crust, followed by two of my favorite ways of serving it.

*serves 6*
1 heaped tablespoon coriander seeds, smashed
1 handful of fresh rosemary, finely chopped
salt and freshly ground black pepper
a light sprinkling of dried oregano
$3^{1}/_{2}$-lb fillet of beef

Pound the coriander seeds in a pestle and mortar, then mix in the rosemary, salt, pepper and oregano and sprinkle on a board. Roll and press the fillet of beef over this, making sure all the mixture sticks to the meat. In a very hot, ridged pan, or on a hot grill, sear the meat for around 5 minutes until brown and slightly crisp on all sides. Remove from the pan. Allow it to rest for 5 minutes, then slice it all up as thinly as you can. Lay the slices on a large plate.

## seared carpaccio of beef with roasted baby beets, creamed horseradish, watercress and Parmesan

*serves 6–8*

1¹⁄₂lb baby beets

olive oil

approximately 10 tablespoons balsamic vinegar

salt and freshly ground black pepper

3¹⁄₂-lb fillet of beef

3¹⁄₂oz freshly grated or prepared horseradish

7oz crème fraîche (about 1 scant cup)

a splash of white wine vinegar

juice of 1 lemon

3 good handfuls of watercress

3¹⁄₂oz shaved Parmesan cheese

Preheat the oven to 450°F. Wash and scrub the beets, trim the ends, and toss into a roasting pan with a little oil, balsamic vinegar and seasoning. Cover with aluminum foil and roast until tender. Cooking time depends on size.

After preparing the beef (see page 175), sprinkle the roasted beets randomly (whole, halved or quartered, depending on size) over the sliced meat. Now mix your horseradish and crème fraîche together. It has to be seasoned well, usually needing a little white wine vinegar or lemon juice. Dribble this over the beets. Dress some watercress with olive oil and lemon juice. Then scatter this, along with some small slivers of shaved Parmesan, all over the plate and get ready to tuck in!

# seared carpaccio of beef with chilli, ginger, radish and soy

This is really good served with crunchy Thai salad (see page 67) and some crusty bread.

*serves 6–8*
3½-lb fillet of beef
1 handful of very finely sliced fresh ginger
    (preferably younger, unstringy roots)
2–3 fresh red or green chillies (or use a mixture of both),
    seeded and finely sliced
1 good handful of radishes, finely sliced
1 small handful of fresh cilantro, leaves picked,
    stalks finely sliced lengthwise
sesame seed oil
soy sauce
juice of 2 limes

After preparing the beef (see page 175), gather your ginger slices and cut finely across into little delicate matchsticks. Flick these randomly over the beef with the chillies, radishes and cilantro. Drizzle with a very small amount of sesame seed oil, some soy sauce and your freshly squeezed lime juice, making sure each slice of meat gets an equal dousing.

# pan-baked pork chops with herby potatoes, parsnips, pears and minted bread sauce

When I make this dish I ask my butcher to slice me a two-rib pork chop. I then ask him to lose one of the ribs and a little of the fat and to push the meat out slightly, leaving me with a huge pork chop that looks fantastic.

*serves 4*
8 pork chops, or 4 double pork chops
1 rosemary, garlic and lemon marinade recipe (page 194)
3 parsnips
3 smooth-skinned pears
1 1/2lb potatoes, scrubbed
salt and freshly ground black pepper
1 minted bread sauce recipe (page 278)

Rub and massage the pork chops with the rosemary marinade and, ideally, refrigerate for 1–6 hours for maximum flavor. Preheat the oven to 425°F. Wash the parsnips and pears and slice into quarters lengthwise, removing the cores from the pears, then cut the potatoes into 1/4-inch-thick pieces. Dry them with paper towels, then put them into an appropriately sized roasting pan with the parsnips, pears, pork chops and the marinade. Toss to lightly coat everything, then season and roast in the oven for 45 minutes to an hour, depending on the size of the chops.

While the chops and veg are cooking, make the minted bread sauce. It's great smeared all over the pork.

# roasted Hamilton poussin wrapped with bacon and stuffed with potatoes and sage

This is nothing to do with the Duke of Hamilton. It's a scrumptious recipe that my handsome art director, Johnny Boy Hamilton, cooks for his lovely wife. Lucky woman. There is something quite cute about the individual chicken thing, and cooking the potatoes in the cavities seems to make them taste even better.

*serves 4*
1lb potatoes, peeled and quartered
sea salt and freshly ground black pepper
4 poussin chickens, or Cornish game hens
1 handful of fresh sage, thyme or rosemary (all are good)
olive oil
about 12 cloves of garlic
12 strips of lean bacon
1 glass of dry white wine

Preheat your oven and an appropriately sized roasting pan to 425°F. Boil your potatoes in salted water until nearly cooked. Drain and allow to cool, then put them in a bowl. Remove any fat from inside of each chicken cavity. Wash and pat dry with paper towels. Season the potatoes with salt and freshly ground black pepper, add your freshly torn herbs and enough olive oil just to coat, and toss. Then stuff your chickens with half your potatoes and herbs. Put them in the hot roasting pan with the garlic and the rest of the potatoes and cook in the preheated oven for 30 minutes. After this time the chicken should be looking as handsome as its inventor and the skin should be crisp and golden. If you are using Cornish game hens larger than poussins, you may need to cook them a bit longer. At this point lay your bacon snugly over the breast meat. Cook for around another 15 minutes.

Remove the chickens from the oven. Take them out of the pan and allow them to rest for 5 minutes while you make a quick bit of gravy. I normally remove as much fat as possible from the pan before placing it on a burner over gentle heat. Splash a glass of white wine into it. Then boil and scrape away all the goodness from the sides of the pan. Simmer this for a couple of minutes. It's not a thick, robust gravy, just a tasty gesture. (A nice option at this point is to add a little cream to the gravy, which works really well.) Served with something nice and green like steamed spinach or chard, and the potatoes pulled out from inside the chickens, it all goes down a treat. Nice one, John.

# fantastic roast chicken

This roast chicken is really tasty. The principle is very similar to the perfect roast chicken recipe in my first book, getting fantastic flavors right into the bird.

*serves 6*
one 2-lb chicken, preferably organic
1 large lemon
8 slices prosciutto or Parma ham, thinly sliced
1–2 cloves of garlic, peeled and finely chopped
2 good handfuls of fresh thyme, leaves picked from stems and finely chopped
salt and freshly ground black pepper
1/2 cup of softened butter
2 1/4lb potatoes, peeled and cut into chunks
1 large celeriac, peeled

Preheat the oven and an appropriately sized roasting pan to 425°F. Wash your chicken inside and out and pat dry with paper towels. Using your fingers, part the breast skin from the breast meat. It's important to try to push your hand gently down the breast, being careful not to rip the skin. With a peeler, remove and chop the fragrant yellow skin of the lemon, keeping the peeled lemon to one side. Then tear up your prosciutto and add to a bowl with the lemon skin, garlic and thyme. Season, and then scrunch it all into the butter. Push this into the space you have made between the meat and the skin—rub and massage any that's left over in and around the bird. It's all tasty stuff. I could tell you to tie the chicken up but I've decided it's a palaver and not worth it in this case. Slash the thigh meat to allow the heat to penetrate a little more, which makes it taste better. Cut the peeled lemon in half and push it into the cavity. Then put your chicken in the hot roasting pan and roast in the preheated oven for 20 minutes.

While the chicken is cooking, parboil the potatoes in salted water for 10 minutes and drain. Cut the celeriac into irregular chunks around the same size as the potatoes. Remove the chicken from the oven, by which time the tasty butter will have melted, flavored and cooked out of the chicken into the bottom of the pan, awaiting your potatoes and celeriac. Normally I put a fork into the cavity of the chicken and lift it out of the tray for 20 seconds while I toss and coat the vegetables in the butter. Put the chicken back on top of the vegetables and cook for around 40 minutes. Leave to stand for 10 minutes. Once the meat and vegetables have been removed, a little light gravy can be made in the pan on the stove with a splash of wine and stock and a little simmering and scraping.

# roasted fillet of beef rolled in herbs and porcini and wrapped in prosciutto

As far as roasted meat goes, this is extremely fast and simple, yet decadently rich. One of the tricks, whether you buy it in a deli or a supermarket, is to ask them to slice your prosciutto and lay it side by side on a large piece of wax paper.

*serves 4*
12–18 slices prosciutto or Parma ham
3 cloves of garlic, peeled
1 good handful of dried porcini, soaked in around 1 cup boiling water
3 very large pats of butter
juice of $1/2$ a lemon
sea salt and freshly ground black pepper
2-lb fillet of beef (preferably from the middle, left whole)
1 good handful of fresh rosemary and thyme, leaves picked from stems and chopped
2 glasses of red wine

Preheat your oven and an appropriately sized roasting pan to 450°F. Make sure there are no gaps in between the laid-out slices of prosciutto on the wax paper. Chop one of the garlic cloves and fry with the soaked porcini in 1 pat of butter for a minute. Then add half of the soaking water (make sure it is grit-free). Simmer slowly and reduce for around 5 minutes before stirring in a squeeze of lemon, the remaining butter and seasoning. Rub your tasty and moist mushrooms over half of the laid-out prosciutto. Season your fillet of beef and roll it in the herbs. Place it on the mushroomy end of the prosciutto and slowly roll up the meat. Once the beef is rolled up, pull off the wax paper and push in the ends of the prosciutto to neaten. Lightly secure with 4 pieces of string. Chefs have a certain way of doing this, but as long as the string holds the meat together I don't care how you do it.

Place the fillet in the hot roasting pan with a couple of cloves of garlic and cook for 25–30 minutes (rare), 40 minutes (medium), 50 minutes (well-done) or 60 minutes (cremated!). Halfway through, add the wine to the pan. When the meat is done, remove it to a chopping board and leave it to rest for 5 minutes. Pour any juices back into the roasting pan. Simmer the juices on top of the stove, scraping all the goodness from the sides of the pan. Remove from the heat and serve as a light red wine gravy. Slice the fillet as thick or as thin as you like and serve with some potatoes or some gorgeous greens. I like to reserve a little of the cooked porcini to serve with sauteed greens.

# braised pigeon breasts with peas, lettuce and scallions

You can use whole pigeons in this recipe, but I prefer to remove the bottom of each carcass with a knife or a pair of scissors to open and flatten them out like a book. The cooking time I have given is sufficient, but if you like your meat pink, then feel free to lessen it.

*serves 4*
4 pigeons (squab)
salt and freshly ground black pepper
olive oil
1 bunch of scallions, green parts chopped and white bulbs left
  whole
1 clove of garlic, peeled and finely chopped
3 very large pats of butter
1 heaped tablespoon flour
1³⁄₄–2lb peas, fresh or frozen
2 heads romaine lettuce, quartered
5 cups chicken or vegetable stock (pages 275–6)

Preheat the oven to 425°F and get a deep casserole or roasting pan hot on the stove. Season the pigeons, then place them skin side down in the hot pan with a little olive oil and cook until lightly golden. Remove from the pan and fry the chopped scallion greens and garlic for 1 minute until slightly softened. Add your butter and the flour. Turn down the heat and cook for a further 3 minutes without coloring. Add your peas, scallion bulbs, lettuce and enough stock to cover, then place the pigeons on top, skin side up. Cook in the preheated oven for 20 minutes. Remove from the oven and allow to sit for 5 minutes before serving.

# Peter's lamb curry

My mate Peter Begg, lovely bloke, fine chef, thoroughbred Scotsman, kilt and no undies, makes the best curry and likes a cold beer. Say no more . . . love him.

*serves 8*

1 hot and fragrant rub recipe (page 195)
2 tablespoons butter
two 14-oz cans of chopped tomatoes
1 cup stock or water
one 3½-lb leg of lamb, diced
1 handful of chopped mint and cilantro
1 cup plain yogurt
salt and freshly ground black pepper
lime juice to taste

*curry paste*

2 inches of fresh ginger, peeled
2 tennis-ball-sized red onions, peeled
10 cloves of garlic, peeled
2 fresh red chillies, with seeds
1 bunch of fresh cilantro

Preheat your oven to 325°F. Lightly toast the hot and fragrant rub mix in the oven or under the broiler. Chop the paste ingredients roughly, add the rub mix and purée in a food processor. In a large casserole, fry the curry paste mixture in the butter until it goes golden, stirring regularly. Add the tomatoes and the stock or water. Bring to the boil, cover with aluminum foil and place in the oven for 1½ hours to intensify the flavors. Remove the foil and continue to simmer on the stove until it thickens. This is your basic curry sauce.

Fry the lamb in a little olive oil until golden, then add to the curry sauce and simmer for around 1 hour or until tender. Feel free to vary the curry by using diced chicken, srhimp or paneer (see below), or vegetables like Swiss chard, spinach, peas, cauliflower, fried eggplant, okra, boiled potatoes, chickpeas or lentils. Sprinkle with chopped cilantro and mint and stir in the yogurt. Season to taste and add a good squeeze of lime juice. Serve with spiced breads, steamed basmati rice and lots and lots of cold beer!

# paneer Indian cheese

In a thick-bottomed pan, bring 2 quarts of heavy cream to the boil, remove from the heat and add a wineglass of white wine vinegar. Stir, then leave for 5 minutes. The milk will begin to curdle. Now pour it through a fine sieve or a colander lined with muslin. Allow the water to drain, then squeeze the remaining curd and chill in the fridge. Chop the cheese into thumb-sized pieces, fry in butter with a little chilli, garlic and sea salt and add to your curry.

## steaks, chops, fillets, legs and breasts, tenderloins, whole birds and half birds, cutlets, noisettes, medallions and all that malarkey

Absolutely everyone cooks these cuts of meat week in, week out. Pork, lamb, beef, chicken: we all cook them. And the idea of the marinades and rubs on pages 194–5 is to give you six possible ways to flavor them—to give you options other than the plain old grilled chop. When you have marinated or rubbed your chosen meat, grill, fry or roast it in a hot oven until perfectly cooked and leave for five minutes before serving.


## marinades and rubs

Each of the following marinades and rubs will make enough to flavor at least six to eight portions of meat or fish. They are a fantastic way of flavoring a piece of meat, taking it in a whole new direction. They're also great tenderizers, helping to break down any tough sinews.

The following flavors are literally the tip of the iceberg. Feel free to vary them depending on what herbs, oils and ingredients you have available. I like to rub and massage the meat for a little while to really get the flavors in there. Sometimes I bash out pork chops so the surface area is a bit bigger, or even lightly score chicken to impregnate them with the flavor quicker. Marinate your meat in the fridge for anything between 1 and 8 hours, but these marinades, when used on first-class pieces of meat, do work best when left all day. I wouldn't leave them for any longer than that. Get your meat in the marinade first thing before work and it will be ready to cook for dinner that night.

Rubs are great ways of simply and cheaply flavoring meat or fish as, generally, they're based around dried herbs and spices, which are nonperishable. You can improvise and make up your own but the three on page 195 are the ones I use all the time.

### Asian marinade

2 stalks of lemongrass, crushed and bruised
1 small handful of kaffir lime leaves, torn
2 tablespoons soy sauce
2 cloves of garlic, crushed
1 thumb-sized piece of ginger, peeled and chopped
1 fresh red chilli, finely chopped
2 limes, halved, juiced and skin squashed
10 good glugs of olive oil

Scrunch the whole lot together in a bowl and coat over your chosen meat. Also works brilliantly with fish.

### yogurt, mint and lime marinade

1 cup of plain organic yogurt
2 good handfuls of fresh mint, chopped
zest and juice of 2 limes
1 tablespoon coriander seeds, crushed
salt and freshly ground black pepper
a couple of glugs of olive oil

Mix together the ingredients and smear over your chosen meat before leaving it to marinate.

### rosemary, garlic and lemon marinade

2 good handfuls of fresh rosemary, pounded
6 cloves of garlic, crushed
10 glugs of olive oil
3 lemons, halved, juiced and skin squashed
freshly ground black pepper

Mix everything together and massage onto your chosen meat. Leave the meat in the marinade until you're ready to cook it.

## hot and fragrant rub

2 tablespoons fennel seeds
2 tablespoons cumin seeds
2 tablespoons coriander seeds
½ tablespoon fenugreek seeds
½ tablespoon black peppercorns
1 clove
½ a cinnamon stick
2 cardamom pods
salt and freshly ground black pepper

Lightly toast all the ingredients in a pan over a gentle heat
before pounding or crushing into a fine powder. This can then
be rubbed generously over your chosen meat.

## fennel seed, thyme and garlic rub

4 tablespoons fennel seeds
2 good handfuls of fresh thyme
2 cloves of garlic
1 bay leaf, ripped
salt and freshly ground black pepper

Pound together and rub all over your chosen meat.

## Cajun spicy rub

2 tablespoons paprika
2 tablespoons cayenne pepper
1 tablespoon black peppercorns, ground
2 cloves of garlic, peeled and crushed
3 tablespoons onion flakes
2 tablespoons dried oregano
salt

Pound all the ingredients together until you have a
powdery consistency and rub all over your chosen meat.

# Botham burger

The good thing about burgers is you can make them thin and big, fat and big, or even turn them into meatballs. In the early days of the Cricketers, the pub where I grew up, I remember my dad used to serve a whopping great burger the size of a cricket ball topped with a huge amount of Cheddar cheese and homemade tomato relish. He very classily called it the Botham burger after the famous cricket pitcher. That's what I love about Essex boys—sheer taste. Feel free to add extra spices if that's what takes your fancy, but here's a really solid basic beefburger recipe. I never thought when I became a chef that I would come back round to respecting the famous beefburger. Unfortunately it hasn't been on the pub's menu for about ten years—what a shame. This might change Dad's mind.

*makes 4 Botham burgers*
2¼lbs ground beef, preferably organic
2 medium red onions, finely chopped
2 large eggs
1–2 handfuls of fresh bread crumbs
1 tablespoon of coriander seeds, crushed
1 small pinch of cumin seeds, crushed
1 heaped teaspoon Dijon mustard
salt and freshly ground black pepper

Preheat the oven to 450°F. Mix and scrunch all the ingredients together. Use the bread crumbs as required to bind and lighten the mixture. Divide into 4, then gently and lightly mold and pack each burger into smallish slightly flattened balls. Place in the oven and roast for 25 minutes, which should leave the middles slightly pink and the outsides nice and crispy. Serve with a grilled bun, a little salad, some gherkins, tomato salsa (page 278), a pint of Guinness and a bottle of ketchup. Howzat!

vegetables

Nothing much has changed in the veg world over the last year and a half, since my first book, but I still believe a lot of good things are going to happen in general supermarkets and markets. I've heard a few rumors that certain supermarkets think they're going to be 90 percent organic by 2005, which is great. I wouldn't worry about price either, because as we buy more produce, grown properly as it used to be before we started cheating and churning it out, it will become nice and cheap so everyone can afford it. Also, the variety of vegetables like cabbages, potatoes and tomatoes, as well as salad greens, is slowly getting better. Things that could only be bought for restaurant use before are now popping up in supermarkets and that's superb.

I have noticed people's curiosity about cooking becoming more intense, which is great. I think a lot of people are now beginning to learn a lot about cooking and are really enjoying it, though sometimes when I walk round the supermarket I see such a massive contrast in buyers and I'm sure that will always be the case. In general I'll see young couples with their carts full of quite interesting vegetables—asparagus, artichokes, arugula—talking and sometimes arguing about the best combinations and ways to cook their veg for dinner. I find it so interesting. Usually they have some really good ideas, but others are definite no-nos and I do feel the urge to go up to them and say, "Excuse me, I'm Dr. Naked Chef, can I possibly help?" But I know they would just turn round and say, "Who are you? On yer bike, mate!" The main thing, though, is that they are interested and they are trying. However, I can never get over the mother with lots of pasty kids and a cart full of Coke, potato chips and canned spaghetti. I feel like kidnapping the kids and force-feeding them vegetables for a month to get some color back into their cheeks. There's no such thing as a vegetable that is too flashy or complicated for a kid. In Italy it is so common to see two-year-olds nibbling on asparagus tips and dipping artichoke hearts in flavored butters and sauces. They love it, it's good fun and it's bloomin' good for them. At the end of the day, their diet is only as good as that of their parents.

## baked endive with thyme, orange juice, garlic and butter

Five years on from swearing that I'd never eat another Belgian endive again, I'm writing a recipe for one that I think is gorgeous. Hypocritical I know, but there you go.

*serves 4*
4 Belgian endive
3 very large pats of butter
1 clove of garlic, peeled and finely chopped
1 good handful of fresh thyme
salt and freshly ground black pepper
approximately 1⅓ cups fresh orange juice

Preheat the oven to 450°F. Remove any discolored outer leaves from the Belgian endive, if need be. Cut in half lengthwise and then quarter each half. In a hot pan, fry the endive with your butter, garlic, thyme and seasoning for about 4 minutes. Add the orange juice and allow to sizzle. Then pour it all into a dish, cover with aluminum foil and bake for 10 minutes. Now remove the foil and bake for a further 10 minutes. Taste and correct your seasoning before serving.

# baked fennel with garlic butter and vermouth

This dish is so quick. I made it the other day, chucked it together and it's really light and flavorsome. It goes fantastically well with any meat or fish.

*serves 4*
3 large heads of fennel
1 clove of garlic, finely sliced
3 large pats of butter
2 wineglasses of dry vermouth (white wine also works)
salt and freshly ground black pepper

Preheat the oven to 425°F. Remove any discolored parts of the fennel, then cut the tops off and slice finely, reserving the feathery leaves. I normally slice each fennel from the top to the root, into about 4 pieces, but it's not that important. You can slice them finer and more delicately if you like. Literally throw all the ingredients except the reserved leaves into a baking dish. Rip off a piece of wax paper, run it under cold water and scrunch it up to make it soft. Then place it snugly over and around the fennel, not the baking dish. This bakes and steams the fennel at the same time—basically making it damn tasty! Cook in the preheated oven for 20 minutes, or until tender. Scatter with the fennel leaves before serving.

# baked field mushrooms studded with garlic and rubbed with butter and pounded thyme

In the restaurant we buy in some fantastic mushrooms, each with its own character, but they are very very expensive. With regard to mushrooms at home, stay a million miles away from the horrible boring button mushroom and go for the flat field mushroom. These vary in size, so I always buy ones as big as coasters. This recipe is absolutely fantastic, juicy and meaty.

*serves 4*
1 good handful of fresh thyme, leaves picked from stems
a pinch of dried chilli
2 cloves of garlic, peeled and finely sliced
juice of 1 lemon
6 good glugs of extra-virgin olive oil
4–8 large flat field mushrooms (such as crimini, portobello
   and shiitake), depending on size
1 large pat of butter
salt and freshly ground black pepper

Preheat your oven to 425°F. Pound your thyme, chilli and a little of the garlic in a pestle and mortar. Squeeze in the lemon juice and add the olive oil. With your hand or a brush, rub the mushrooms all over with this mixture. Make sure all the flavored oil is used up. Tightly pack the mushrooms together, bottom-side up, in an ovenproof dish or roasting pan, and with a knife make 2 to 3 little slits randomly over each one. Insert a slice of the remaining garlic into each slit. Dot the butter over the mushrooms, season, and bake for around 15–25 minutes—cooking time depends on the size of your mushrooms—until soft, slightly colored and damn juicy. Taste one and see. Great served with steak and French fries, ripped into a warm salad, chopped into ravioli, sliced and tossed with pasta and a bit of cream . . . nice one.

# baked Jerusalem artichokes, bread crumbs, thyme and lemon

This dish is absolutely spanking in the middle of your table with a Sunday roast or with a grilled bit of chicken or a pork chop. The bread crumbs and thyme become crispy on top, giving the dish a really sexy texture of soft artichoke and crisp topping.

*serves 4–6*
1 1/3 cups heavy cream or crème fraîche
juice of 1 lemon
2 cloves of garlic, peeled and finely chopped
1 good handful of fresh thyme, leaves picked from stems
    and chopped
3 handfuls of grated Parmesan cheese
salt and freshly ground black pepper
2 1/4 lbs Jerusalem artichokes, peeled and sliced
    as thick as a pencil
2 good handfuls of fresh bread crumbs
olive oil

Preheat your oven to 425°F. In a bowl mix your cream, lemon juice, garlic, half the thyme and most of the Parmesan, and season well to taste. Throw in the sliced Jerusalem artichokes. Mix well and place everything in an ovenproof baking dish.

Mix the bread crumbs with the rest of the thyme and Parmesan and some salt and pepper. Sprinkle all the flavored bread crumbs over the artichokes and drizzle with a little olive oil. Bake in the oven for around 30 minutes, until the artichokes are tender and the bread crumbs are golden.

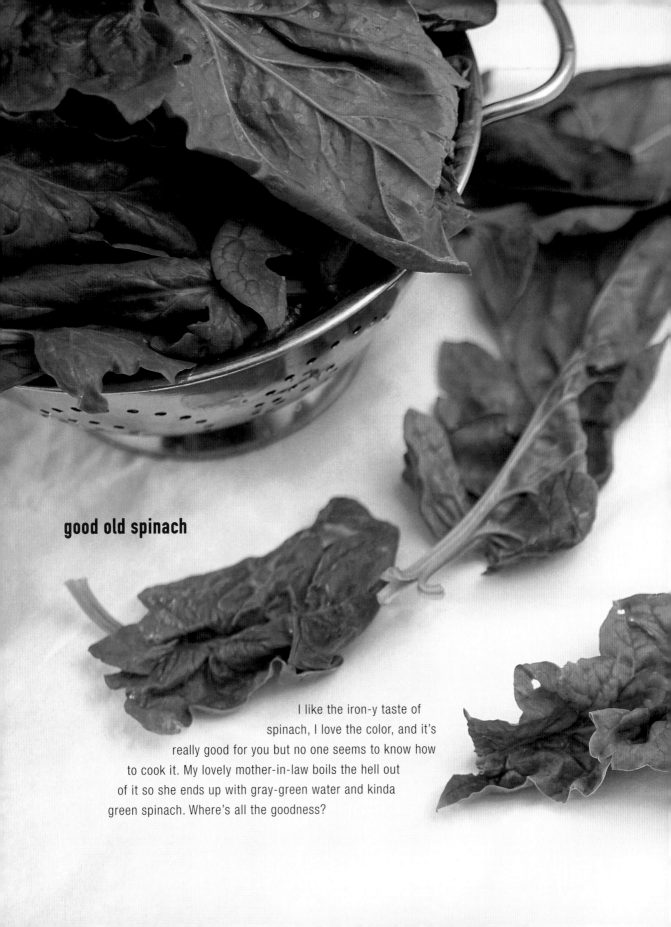

**good old spinach**

I like the iron-y taste of
spinach, I love the color, and it's
really good for you but no one seems to know how
to cook it. My lovely mother-in-law boils the hell out
of it so she ends up with gray-green water and kinda
green spinach. Where's all the goodness?

In the water. So forget everything you know about cooking spinach, this is the way we do it from now on. Either pick or buy spinach on the stalk, which you should wash well, sometimes two or three times but that's not the end of the world. If you've got lovely young leaves, then leave them on the stalk and just pick the outer leaves off. Or, as most of us do, buy packs of prewashed baby spinach from the supermarket—how convenient. Here are four brilliant ways with spinach. You can also use Swiss chard or Savoy cabbage in place of spinach.

## the simplest spinach with nutmeg and butter

*serves 4*

To a hot pan or wok add a little oil, sway the pan about and add 4 huge handfuls of spinach. This will look like a lot, but it will soon cook down. It will sizzle a bit so just stand by it and turn it over every 5 seconds. After about 30 seconds it will begin to wilt and hopefully only a little water will start to cook out of the spinach (if there is a lot, then pour a little away). Add 3 big pats of butter and grate in about 12 rubs of nutmeg to taste. Mix, season and serve. The butter and the water should mix together, giving you just enough natural sauce to bind everything together.

## spinach and porcini with rosemary and lemon

*serves 4*

Dried porcini are everywhere now—too expensive, but the flavor is extreme and extraordinary. A small package is more than enough for this recipe. Just cover the porcini with boiling water and soak for 15 minutes. Keeping the soaking liquid to one side, fry the mushrooms with 2 large pats of butter, 1 chopped clove of garlic and around 1 tablespoon of finely chopped rosemary. Fry for 4 minutes and then gently pour in around half of the soaking liquid— I say gently because sometimes a little grit falls to the bottom, which you don't want. Simmer the mushrooms until the butter and liquor have reduced just to coat them. Then plonk in 4 huge handfuls of spinach and mix until the spinach is vibrant green and wilted. Season to taste with a squeeze of lemon, salt and freshly ground black pepper. An excellent filling for vegetarian cannelloni with a little ricotta.

## scallions, sweet peas, white wine and spinach

*serves 4*

In a pot slowly fry a handful of finely chopped scallions for a couple of minutes in a glug of olive oil and a pat of butter. Then add 2 handfuls of fresh or frozen peas and cook for another couple of minutes before adding a good glass of dry white wine. Bring to the boil and simmer for a few minutes before adding 4 huge handfuls of spinach. Turn this over and cook until the spinach is wilted. Add 2 huge pats of butter and season well to taste.

## steamed spinach with coconut rice

*serves 4*
one 14-oz can of coconut milk
salt
14oz long-grain rice
4 tablespoons soy sauce
2 tablespoons olive oil
4 handfuls of baby spinach, washed

Place the coconut milk in a pan and top up with enough water to cook the rice in. Bring to the boil, add a pinch of salt and the rice. Cook until the rice is tender, then drain in a colander. Pour a little more water into the pan and put it back on the heat. Place the colander over the pan and simmer the water to steam the rice, making it light and fluffy. Place in a warm serving bowl, add the soy sauce and olive oil and stir in the spinach. The heat from the rice will cook the spinach in a matter of minutes, keeping it lovely and green and retaining all its goodness.

# good old mashed veg

This is a gutsy veg dish which just about everyone loves. My missus makes me fantastic mashed vegetables, beautifully seasoned and drizzled with olive oil—the only thing is, they are meant to be separate servings of boiled carrots and new potatoes! So if you, too, are prone to overcooking your veg, just mash it all together.

*serves 4*
4½lb root vegetables (celeriac, potatoes,
    rutabaga, parsnips, carrots, Jerusalem artichokes)
salt and freshly ground black pepper
extra-virgin olive oil or butter

Feel free to use any single vegetable or a mixture of your favorites. Simply peel them, chop them up into golf-ball-sized pieces, place in salted boiling water and cook until nice and tender. Drain in a colander before placing the veg back in the pan and mashing with a potato masher. Make it as smooth or as chunky as you like. Season carefully, then enrich the flavor with extra-virgin olive oil or butter, or both, to taste.

Once cooked, the mash can be kept warm in a bowl covered with aluminum foil over simmering water. This is handy when cooking for a dinner party, as you can get one lot of veg done and nicely out of the way.

# baked beets with balsamic vinegar, marjoram and garlic

A fantastic veg that is great served with white fish such as grilled monkfish, or with beef carpaccio (see page 175), or as part of an antipasto plate along with some tasty beans, sliced prosciutto and tomato-rubbed crostini. If you're lucky enough to buy beets with their leaves, remove them, keep them and use like spinach—they taste amazing.

*serves 4*
1lb fresh raw beets, preferably golf-ball size, scrubbed
10 cloves of garlic, unpeeled and squashed
1 handful of fresh marjoram or sweet oregano, leaves picked from
   stems
salt and freshly ground black pepper
10 tablespoons balsamic vinegar
6 tablespoons extra-virgin olive oil

Preheat the oven to 400°F. Tear off around 5 ft. of aluminum foil and fold it in half to give you double thickness. If you can only get larger beets halve them to speed up their cooking time, otherwise use them whole. Place them in the middle of the foil with the garlic and marjoram, season generously with salt and freshly ground black pepper, then fold the sides in to the middle. Before you seal the foil, add the vinegar and olive oil. Scrunch or fold the foil together to seal at the top. Put on a baking sheet and place in the preheated oven and cook for around 1 hour, until tender. Serve in the bag at the table—lovely.

# baked carrots with cumin, thyme, butter and Chardonnay

I love this dish made with baby carrots, but feel free to use fat old ones sliced at an angle if you please. Butter and wine make a fantastic sauce, which just makes it for me. Serve with anything you like.

*serves 4*
1lb baby carrots, preferably organic, scrubbed and
   left whole
$1/2$ teaspoon cumin seeds, crushed
1 handful of fresh thyme leaves
4 large pats of butter
1 glass of Chardonnay
salt and freshly ground black pepper

Preheat the oven to 425°F. Tear off around 5 ft. of aluminum foil and fold it in half to give you double thickness. Place everything but the wine and seasoning in the middle of the foil. Bring up the sides and pour in the white wine. Season well. Fold or scrunch the foil together to seal. Cook in the preheated oven for 45 minutes until the carrots are tender. You may need to cook for longer if the carrots are bigger than baby ones.

# bread

# basic bread recipe

1oz fresh yeast or $^3/_4$oz active dried yeast (three $^1/_4$-oz packages)
2 tablespoons honey (or sugar)
just over 2 cups tepid water
just over 2lb bread flour (6 to 8 cups)
2 tablespoons salt
some extra flour for dusting

*Stage 1*

Dissolve the yeast and honey (or sugar) in half the tepid water.

*Stage 2*

On a clean surface or in a large bowl, make a pile of the flour and salt. Make a well in the center and pour in all the dissolved yeast mixture. With 4 fingers of one hand, make circular movements from the center moving outward, slowly bringing in more and more of the flour until all the yeast mixture is soaked up. Then pour the other half of the tepid water into the center and gradually incorporate all the flour to make a moist dough. (Certain flours may need a little more water, so don't be afraid to adjust the quantities.)

*Stage 3*

Kneading! This is the best bit, just rolling, pushing and folding the dough over and over for 5 minutes. This develops the gluten and the structure of the dough. If any of the dough sticks to your hands, just rub them together with a little extra flour.

*Stage 4*

Flour both your hands well, and lightly flour the top of the dough. Make it into a roundish shape and place on a baking tray. Deeply score the dough with a knife—allowing it to relax and proof (rise) with ease. Leave it to rise until it's doubled in size. Ideally you want a warm, moist, draft-free place for the quickest rise, for example near a warm stove, or just in a warm room, and you can even cover it with plastic wrap if you want to speed things up. This proofing process improves the flavor and texture of the dough and should take around 40 minutes, depending on the conditions.

When the dough has doubled in size you need to punch the air out of it by bashing it around for a minute. Now you can shape it into whatever shape is required—round, flat, filled, in a loaf pan or whatever—and leave it to rise for a second time until it doubles in size again. The important thing is not to lose your confidence now. Don't feel a need to rush through this, because the second proofing will give you the lovely, delicate soft texture that we all love in fresh bread.

Now it's time to cook your loaf. After all your hard work, don't spoil your efforts. You want to keep all the air inside the loaf, so don't knock it. Gently place it in the preheated oven, don't slam the door. Bake according to the time and temperature given in the recipe variations which follow. You can tell if your bread is cooked by tapping its bottom (if it's in a baking pan you'll have to take it out). If it sounds hollow it's cooked, if it doesn't then pop it back in for a little longer. Place it on a rack to cool. You're going to love this bread!

# chocolate twister bread

1 basic bread recipe (pages 222–3)
3/4 cup plus 2 tablespoons soft butter
7oz hazelnuts, lightly roasted and crushed or broken up
11oz semisweet or bittersweet chocolate (70% cocoa),
   the best you can get, chopped up or grated

At Stage 5 of the basic recipe, divide the dough into 2 equal parts. After the second rising, take each piece of dough and push out into a squarish shape on a floured board. Then roll out to about 7 inches wide. At this point, roll the other way and keep rolling to achieve a long rectangle about 1/4 inch thick—it doesn't have to be exact. Using a knife, spread the butter thinly across the dough. Sprinkle over the hazelnuts and chocolate and roll up across the width like a jelly roll. Cut across into 1-inch-wide slices. Place the slices next to each other on a greased baking sheet, cut side upward, with small gaps in between. Bake in a preheated 400°F oven for around 20 minutes. Allow to cool for 20 minutes before eating with a glass of cold milk.

# fruit loaf

Don't worry if you haven't got a pan to make this in. Simply shape into a round, place on a flour-dusted baking sheet and score in a criss-cross fashion.

1 basic bread recipe (pages 222–3)
a pinch of ground cinnamon
1 clove, ground
7oz dried apricots
3³/₄oz dried dates
7oz dried raisins

Place the spices and fruit in a food processor or chop very finely. Scrunch into the dough mixture at Stage 2 of the basic recipe, possibly holding back a little water from the recipe, as residual water in dried fruit varies. Once you have a good bread consistency, carry on as normal until Stage 5.

After punching all the air out of the dough, pack it into an appropriately sized greased and floured bread pan. The dough should just underfill the pan, so at the end of Stage 5, when it rises for the second time, the bread will have doubled in size and will be a whopping great light and fruity blooming bloomer. Lovely. Bake in a preheated oven for around 50 minutes at 400°F, then remove from the pan and put the loaf back in the oven, resting directly on the oven rack, for a final 10 minutes until it sounds hollow when tapped. Allow to cool for 30 minutes.

# Gennaro bread

This is a bread very similar to one my mate Gennaro used to make with the leftover, slightly dried-up, unwanted cheese and remaining prosciutto. The bread looks fantastic baked in unglazed, clean little terra-cotta pots but, quite frankly, you can cook this bread as rolls or as a loaf. Adjust the cooking time accordingly.

1 basic bread recipe (pages 222–3)
14oz mixed cheese (use Parmesan, fontina, taleggio
    and a little Gorgonzola), grated or broken up
4 large egg yolks
10 slices of prosciutto, torn up
1 handful of fresh basil, torn

At Stage 2 of the basic recipe, mix in all the ingredients and carry on through to Stage 5, when you should divide your bread dough into 6 balls. I like to put them into 6 small, greased and floured terra-cotta plant pots. Flour the top and allow to rise until doubled in size. Carefully transfer to the preheated oven and bake for around 30 minutes at 425°F.

# pizzas

Pizza crusts are great to make, as they only need to rise once. The recipe below makes enough for 4 pizza crusts. Top with one of my 3 suggested toppings or some of your own favorite ones.

*pizza base*
1 basic bread recipe (pages 222–3)

At Stage 5 of the basic recipe, divide your dough into 4 pieces and simply roll each into a large, plate-sized, slightly irregular round shape about ¼ inch thick, using a rolling pin. Once you've added your chosen topping, place the pizza directly onto the rack of your preheated oven and bake for around 5–7 minutes at 475°F until the topping has melted and the pizza crust is lightly golden.

## olive, tomato, arugula, Parmesan and mozzarella pizza

Halve and seed 8 ripe plum tomatoes and dice them. Place in a bowl with 2 good handfuls of pitted olives. Season with salt and freshly ground black pepper, a touch of olive oil and a splash of red wine vinegar. Smear this onto each pizza crust, then sprinkle with pieces of mozzarella. Bake as above, then remove from the oven and sprinkle with some lightly dressed arugula and a good shaving of Parmesan cheese.

## mushroom, mozzarella, thyme and spicy sausage meat pizza

Slice up 6 fat mushrooms (cremini, portobello, or shiitake, for instance) and fry with a good handful of fresh thyme and some chopped garlic in a little olive oil until golden. Season well with salt and freshly ground black pepper and remove from the heat. Add a little extra olive oil and smear the mushrooms evenly over each pizza crust. Split the skins of 4 spicy sausages and sprinkle very small pieces of the meat on top of the mushrooms. Scatter with a little chopped fresh chilli, add a little mozzarella or other melting cheese—taleggio or fontina—and bake in the oven as above.

## mozzarella, prosciutto and basil pizza

Rub your pizza crusts with olive oil and randomly scatter with pieces of buffalo mozzarella. Rip over some fresh basil and 2 or 3 nice slices of prosciutto or Parma ham. Bake in the oven as above and serve grated with fresh Parmesan.

# chickpea Moroccan flatbread

A very quick bread to make as it only needs one rising. Great for filling with salad, salsas and grilled meats, and especially tasty cooked on grills. Also great served with all the tapas recipes (pages 36–51).

1 basic bread recipe (pages 222–3)
1 tablespoon of cumin seeds, lightly cracked
1 tablespoon of coriander seeds, lightly cracked
one 14-oz can of chickpeas, drained and mashed

At Stage 2 of the basic recipe, mix in the cumin seeds, coriander seeds and chickpeas and carry on through the recipe as normal until Stage 5, when you should divide your batch of dough into 10 pieces. Roll out each of these to ¼ inch thick and gently pull out into a slightly irregular oval shape. Cook 1 or 2 at a time, depending on how big your oven is, straight away without a second rising, directly on the rack of the preheated oven at 450°F. They take about 4 minutes to cook and puff up beyond belief. Allow to cool slightly for a couple of minutes before eating.

## slashed cheese, chilli and paprika flatbread

Great with salads and salami. Oh, and roast chicken.

1 basic bread recipe (pages 222–3)
5½oz goat's cheese, broken up
5½oz fresh Parmesan cheese, grated
1 heaped tablespoon paprika
4–6 dried red chillies, crumbled

Add all the ingredients at Stage 2 of the basic recipe, then carry on through to Stage 5, when, after punching out the air, you should divide the bread into 2 pieces and roll them out in an irregular elongated triangle shape, about ¾ inch thick. Slash the bread about 5 or 6 times and stretch it open to expose the gaps. Place on a large baking sheet and allow to rise for around 20 minutes before baking in a preheated oven at 425°F for 15–20 minutes until golden. Allow to cool for 10 minutes before eating.

desserts

You little tiger. Naughty but nice. I can't, I can't, I can't . . . oooh, go on then. We always try to say no to dessert but, quite frankly, if you want it, have it. I'm sure I'll be quoted on this in ten years' time when I've got a workman's bum and giant love handles! Desserts aren't always fattening or unhealthy, but if you feel guilty after eating them, then walk up the stairs instead of taking the elevator, that's my philosophy. This is a small collection of tasty and very simple desserts—not technical or massively precise, which is the kind of vibe I think most people like at home, as opposed to being in my commercial kitchen.

## orange and polenta biscuits

Extremely simple and slightly unusual cookie-type biscuits, with the polenta giving a fantastic crunch. Great with ice cream, chocolatey things or simply with a cup of coffee.

*makes around 25 biscuits*
3/4 cup butter
2/3 cup sugar
9oz polenta
all-purpose flour
zest of 2–3 oranges, finely chopped
2 large eggs

Rub the butter, sugar, polenta and flour together before mixing in the orange zest and the eggs. Cover with plastic wrap and put in the fridge for an hour, until slightly firm. Place a large square of wax paper on a baking sheet and spoon small teaspoons of the mixture in lines 2 inches apart. Bake in a preheated oven at 375°F for around 5–6 minutes until the outside edges of your biscuits are lightly golden. Remove from the oven and allow to cool for 15 minutes before eating.

# chocolate pots

The beauty of this dessert is that it is so smooth, silky and rich. However, if you want to lighten the texture to make it into more of a mousse, then follow the recipe here but fold in 2 stiffly whipped egg whites before pouring into the pots. Small servings are the key—I generally use espresso cups as they're the ideal size. Chocolate pots are brilliant for dinner parties as you can make them the day before and stick them in the fridge until needed. They are ideal served with the orange and polenta biscuits on page 241.

*serves 4*
1 cup light cream
7oz best-quality semisweet or bittersweet chocolate (70% cocoa solids)
2 large egg yolks
3 tablespoons brandy, the best you can get
1 tablespoon plus 2 teaspoons butter

In a thick-bottomed pan, heat the cream until nearly boiling. Remove and set aside for 1 minute before snapping in your chocolate. Stir in until melted and smooth. Once melted, beat in your egg yolks and brandy and stir until smooth. Allow to cool slightly before stirring in the butter until the mixture is smooth. Pour into individual serving pots.

P.S. Sometimes if you add the butter when the chocolate isn't cool enough it will make the chocolate look as if it has split. To rectify this, allow the mixture to cool a little longer before whisking in a little cold milk until you have a smooth consistency again.

# two-nuts chocolate torte

This is the best chocolate nut thang around. The day after you should try crumbling it over some ice cream with a little espresso poured over the top. I always bake this torte in a cheesecake or springform pan or I make small ones baked in those pans you can use for mince pies, but you can use any well-greased and floured cake pan.

*serves 8*
5½oz shelled and peeled almonds
5½oz shelled walnuts, finely ground
11oz best-quality semisweet or bittersweet chocolate (70% cocoa solids)
1 heaped teaspoon best-quality unsweetened cocoa powder
1 cup plus 2 tablespoons butter
½ cup superfine sugar
6 large eggs, separated
salt

Preheat the oven to 375°F. Line the bottom of a 8- or 10-inch pie plate with a piece of wax paper before buttering the bottom and sides then dusting with flour. Place the nuts into a food processor and whizz up until finely ground. Then add the chocolate and cocoa and whizz for 30 seconds to break up the chocolate. Put to one side in a separate bowl. Add the butter and sugar to the food processor and process until pale and fluffy. At this point add the egg yolks one at a time, then mix together with the chocolate and nuts.

In another bowl beat the egg whites with a pinch of salt until they form stiff peaks. Gently fold the egg whites into the chocolate, butter and nut mix. Pour all the mixture into the pie plate. Bake in the preheated oven for around an hour. To test if the torte is cooked, insert a toothpick or the tip of a knife for 5 seconds; when removed it should be reasonably clean. Serve with whipped cream, ice cream or crème fraîche.

# a kinda Portuguese custard pie

After eating some fantastic Portuguese cream tarts I was baffled by the crisp, light and almost chewy pastry. I tried to find out the secret to making the pastry but had no luck. So I have come up with a cunning plan to imitate it, which I think is fantastic. I found the filling kinda boring, so I've tweaked it to give it a bit of life. Might look like a pain in the butt but is in fact the quickest custard pie around.

*makes around 16 pastry cases*

*pastry*
approximately a 9-oz slab of puff pastry
1 large egg yolk
4 tablespoons superfine sugar
a light grating of nutmeg
a couple of pinches of cinnamon

Dust a surface with flour and roll out your pastry to a bit bigger than a 9 x 11 inch piece of paper. Brush with the egg yolk and scatter the rest of the ingredients over, being subtle with the nutmeg and cinnamon. Roll the pastry up tightly like a jelly roll to make a long sausage shape. With a knife, cut across the sausage into 1-inch pieces. Take 8 pieces aside and freeze the rest of the pastry for a rainy day.

Preheat the oven to 400°F. Turn all the pieces of pastry swirl-side up and flatten them slightly. Dust the work surface and your pastry with flour, then roll each piece out into a thin circle (around the size of a teacup saucer). Even I don't have proper pastry molds at home, so I just grease and flour the outsides of 8 of my sturdy glass tumblers. Then I place a circle of pastry on top of each tumbler, pleating, pinching and hugging the pastry around them. Place the tumblers on a baking tray, pastry at the top, and put in the preheated oven for around 15 minutes, until crisp and golden.

Remove from the oven and, while still hot, take a kitchen towel and pat the slightly raised top of the pastry back down onto the flat bottom of the tumbler—giving you a flat base again. Allow to cool and carefully remove the pastry cases from around the tumblers. Fill your pastry cases with the custard filling (page 248).

*makes enough to fill 8 pastry cases*

*custard*
6 large eggs
4 generous teaspoons good runny honey
2 vanilla beans, scored lengthwise and seeds removed
zest of 1 orange
2¹/₂ cups heavy cream

Whip up the eggs, honey, vanilla seeds and orange zest in a bowl. (Don't waste the vanilla pods; simply pop them in a jar with some sugar to make a tasty vanilla sugar.) At the same time, in a thick-bottomed pan, heat the cream until nearly boiling. Add it immediately to the rest of the ingredients in the bowl, while whipping fast with a whisk for 30 seconds. Add the mixture back to the pan over medium heat, stirring continuously and using a spatula to get into the edges. This is a very quick and almost aggressive method of cooking a thick egg custard—which is normally done in a bowl over simmering water or in the oven in a bain-marie, like a brûlée—so keep stirring to keep your custard smooth. When it gets as thick as thick yogurt, spoon it into your pastry cases and allow to cool. A skin will begin to form on the top of each pie. To finish them off, make a little caramel . . .

*caramel*
1 big handful of superfine sugar
3 tablespoons of water

Place the sugar and water in a pan. Bring to the boil and gently agitate until golden brown. At this point it will be hotter than hot—*don't even think about tasting it*. No kids allowed. Dribble the mixture randomly over your custard tarts—it will bubble and cool to a crisp caramel. Fantastic. Oh yeah—place the pan in the sink and half fill with water before boiling it again—you'll have no grief washing it up.

# crème brûlée the way I like it

I have eaten crème brûlées all over the gaff and, at the end of the day, an egg custard is an egg custard. Some are good and some are overcooked and bad, but the most important thing is that the custard should be only an inch thick, with a lovely crisp layer of thin caramel on top. So many people plonk their custard mix into a deep ramekin dish with a fat layer of hard caramel on top and that's just not right.

*serves 6*
11oz fresh rhubarb
3 tablespoons superfine sugar
2 vanilla beans
1½ cups minus 2 tablespoons heavy cream
1 cup minus 2 tablespoons whole milk
8 large egg yolks
⅓ cup granulated sugar

Preheat the oven to 275°F. Roughly slice up the rhubarb and place it in a pan with the superfine sugar and 5 tablespoons of water. Simmer until tender, divide among 6 small serving dishes which your brûlée will be cooked in, then set aside.

Score the vanilla pods lengthwise and run the knife up the pod to remove the vanilla seeds. Scrape these into the pan with the pods, cream and milk and slowly bring to a boil. Meanwhile beat together the yolks and the granulated sugar in a bowl until light and fluffy. When the cream and milk are just boiling, remove the vanilla pods and add little by little to the egg mixture, whisking continuously. I like to remove any bubbles or froth from the mixture before dividing it into the serving dishes, on top of the rhubarb. Stand these in an appropriately sized roasting pan filled with water halfway up the containers, and bake in the preheated oven for around 25 minutes until the custard mixture has set but is still slightly wobbly in the center.

Allow to cool to room temperature, then place in the fridge until ready to serve. Sprinkle with more granulated sugar and caramelize under a very hot broiler or using a kitchen blowtorch. Lovely.

# Sheila's pudding

This is a variation of the classic Eve's pudding which uses stewed apples. I love peaches for this pudding, though many fruits can be used, such as rhubarb with almonds or plums on their own. I called it Sheila's pudding for a laugh really . . . I'm a strange boy.

*serves 6*

6 ripe peaches or nectarines, halved and pits removed
4 heaped teaspoons demerara or brown granulated sugar
1 vanilla bean, scored lengthwise and seeds removed
½ cup plus 1 tablespoon butter
½ cup superfine sugar
2 large free-range eggs
1 cup self-rising flour

Preheat the oven to 350°F. Put the peaches in a saucepan with the demerara sugar, the vanilla seeds and 4 tablespoons of water. Simmer for 5 minutes and then place into a well-greased and lightly floured ovenproof dish or bowl. Beat together the butter, superfine sugar and eggs until light and fluffy. Add the flour, mix thoroughly and spread over the peaches.

Bake in the preheated oven for 45 minutes. Remove from the oven and serve with hot custard or something cold, like vanilla ice cream or crème fraîche.

## party cake

3 rounded tablespoons unsweetened
    cocoa powder
1 cup sugar
3/4 cup plus 2 tablespoons butter
3 large eggs, preferably free-range
1 1/3 cups self-rising flour, sifted
1 rounded teaspoon baking powder
1 handful of flaked almonds
1 cup minus 2 tablespoons heavy cream

1 large handful of raspberries
1 large handful of strawberries

*chocolate topping*
6 tablespoons plus 2 teaspoons butter
3 3/4 oz best semisweet or bittersweet
    chocolate
1 cup confectioners' sugar
3 tablespoons milk

Preheat the oven to 350°F. Line the bases of two 8-inch round cake pans with greased wax paper. Mix the cocoa powder with 4 tablespoons of boiling water until smooth. In a separate bowl, beat the sugar and butter until fluffy, add the cocoa mixture, eggs, flour and baking powder. Mix well, fold in the nuts. Divide the mixture between the pans. Bake for about 25 minutes. When cooked, allow to cool, then remove from the pans.

Melt the chocolate topping ingredients in a bowl over some lightly simmering water. Stir until blended well and allow to cool. Whip the heavy cream to soft peaks and sweeten with a little sugar to taste. To assemble the cake, remove the wax paper from both cake layers. Drizzle each one with a little sherry if you like. Spread the cream over one of the layers, then sprinkle the fruit on top. Sandwich the second layer on top and press down. Run a knife around the edge of the cake to smooth it off and drizzle over your chocolate topping. Happy days, you've done it! But allow the chocolate topping to firm up slightly before tucking in.

paros

# strawberries marinated in balsamic vinegar

*serves 4*
2–3 big pints of strawberries, sliced if large
approximately 5 tablespoons sugar, to taste
10 tablespoons balsamic vinegar
1 vanilla bean, scored lengthwise and seeds removed
14oz mascarpone cheese
4 or 5 leaves of fresh mint or basil, finely sliced

When the strawberries taste pukka and are juicy like they should be, pinch off the stems, place in a bowl and scatter generously with the sugar followed by the balsamic vinegar. Stir around and allow to marinate for up to 2 hours. Mix the vanilla seeds with the mascarpone cheese and sweeten to taste with a little sugar. Don't forget you can use the vanilla pod to flavor a small jar of sugar. Place a big lob of mascarpone on a plate covered with a generous heap of strawberries and the tasty balsamic juice. A fine scattering of mint or basil will freshen it slightly.

P.S. If you find you have any leftover strawberries and marinade, squash it all up, freeze for 2½ hours and you've got a lovely frappé (see page 261).

## malted milk balls and ice cream

*serves 4*
2 packets of malted milk balls
a tub of good vanilla ice cream

Bash malted milk balls and sprinkle over a generous serving of vanilla ice cream.

# Campari and passionfruit sorbet

*serves 4*
1 cup water
1 cup sugar
15 passionfruit
1 wineglass of Campari

Place the water and sugar in a pan, bring to the boil and simmer for 5 minutes. Remove from the heat and allow to cool for a while. Halve your passionfruit and scoop out the flesh, seeds and juice using a spoon. Stir this up—you can pass it through a coarse sieve to remove the seeds, but quite frankly I think that's a palaver. I like the seeds. Mix the passionfruit with the Campari and sugar syrup in a plastic tub or earthenware dish and place in the freezer. Generally, sorbet takes 2 hours to set. Try to stir it around every half an hour if you remember. Serve on its own, with some seasonal fruit, or in a cone with some vanilla ice cream.

# pineapple and grapefruit frappé

This recipe works with just about any fruit or combination of your choice because the principle is so basic. A frappé is basically a cross between a granita (like an icy Slush Puppy) and a smooth sorbet. As both pineapples and grapefruits can vary so much in natural sweetness, add the sugar to your own taste.

*serves 4*
2 ripe pineapples, peeled and roughly chopped
3 grapefruits, halved and juiced
sugar to taste

Whizz up the pineapple in a blender until smooth and pass through a coarse sieve. Add the grapefruit juice and stir in sugar to taste, remembering that the sweetness from the sugar will lessen slightly when frozen, so use a touch more than you normally would. Place in the freezer for around $2\frac{1}{2}$ hours to set, stirring every 45 minutes.

bevvies

me

peter

ben

When I first moved to London in 1992 all I heard with regard to cocktails and fine drinks was "Dick Bradsell this," "Dick Bradsell that." His name cropped up so often I thought he was a film star. Having trained at Zanzibar in London, his precision and natural flair for mixing cocktails, and his obvious ability to evolve his drinks in new ventures, led to him setting up many great cocktail bars. With his name behind Dick's Bar at the Atlantic in Piccadilly, he also set up bars at the Soho Brasserie, the Moscow Club, the Café de Paris, Fred's Club, the Player, the Flamingo and, most recently, Match Bar—all in London.

It wasn't until five years later that I had the pleasure of meeting him at the Player—he shook my hand and gave me one of the most memorable drinks I'd ever drunk. It sounds over the top from someone who knows nothing about cocktails, but it was bloomin' fantastic. He spoke to me for five minutes. In that time he made me realize that cocktail-making is no different from cooking. When I say this, what I mean is that sometimes there are measurements and guidelines but a lot of the time it is open to innovation and natural flair. I was blown away by the way he described making drinks—his eyes lit up and his animated body language said it all to me. Passion.

I hadn't spoken to Dick again until I was thinking about having this bevvies section in my book. Personally, I thought he was the only person for the job and I knew he'd do us all proud. So we sat down together and have come up with a whole range of drinks for you that can easily be made at home. All of the spirits and liqueurs mentioned can be bought from any good liquor store at a reasonable price.

dick

## dry Martini

There are so many different ways of making this and, just for us, Dick has come up with a "naked" Martini in the "Franklin Style," which means it's poured straight from the freezer without being stirred over ice in the traditional way. It's named after Franklin D. Roosevelt, who preferred to have 2 olives in his.

*naked*
Take a frozen cocktail glass from the freezer, put a couple of drops of dry vermouth into the glass and top with freezing-cold vodka or gin. Add 2 olives.

*stirred*
Fill a pitcher with ice, splash on some vermouth, stir and then discard the liquid. Your ice is now coated with vermouth. Add 3 ounces of gin or vodka to this and stir as many times as you like. Strain into a prechilled glass before garnishing with an olive or a twist of lemon.

*shaken*
You can shake a Martini but the result will be a cloudy drink with little bits of broken ice on top. The cocktail of choice for James Bond, of course.

## Tom Collins

The original Tom Collins employed sweet Old Tom gin, but unfortunately this is now only available in the Far East. If using London dry gin the drink is a John Collins. The vodka version is conveniently known as a Vodka Collins. Shaking a Collins and pouring it neat into a glass then adding soda water creates a Gin Fizz. And a Sling was originally the basic Collins recipe made with plain water—definitely one of the earliest of cocktails. To make the sugar syrup, mix an equal amount of sugar and boiling water together and stir until clear.

Into a shaker pour 2 ounces of gin, 2 tablespoons of fresh lemon juice and 3 teaspoons of sugar syrup. Shake with ice and then strain over fresh ice in a tumbler. Fill to the top with soda water and stir. Garnish with a lemon slice and a cherry.

## old fashioned

This is a drink for purists. It needs a very good-quality spirit, so Dick suggests using Wild Turkey or Maker's Mark bourbon, Cockspur, Mount Gay or Myers rum and any decent brandy. The idea is to take a dark spirit like brandy, bourbon or rum and bring out its natural depth of flavor; you sweeten it, then give it depth by adding bitters. Perform the same ritual each time you make this and you'll get it right every time.

Take an old-fashioned glass like a whisky tumbler and pour in 4 drops of bitters and 2 teaspoons of sugar syrup (although this depends on the sweetness of your chosen spirit—brandy needs more, rum needs less). See the Tom Collins recipe on page 266 for a note about making sugar syrup. Then add 2 ice cubes and stir. Add 2 more ice cubes, 1 ounce of your preferred spirit and stir. Then 2 more ice cubes and a further 1 ounce of your spirit. Stir. Then more ice and stir again. The alcohol should now fill your glass as the ice has diluted it. Garnish with a twist of orange or lemon—lemon being particularly good with rum.

## Bellini

This is the famous drink from Harry's Bar in Venice, where they have a monopoly on the best peaches in the world. Over there they use the local Italian sparkling wine called prosecco. The drink tastes far better when you use this fizz, so try to get hold of some. Rather than being served in a champagne glass, the original was served in a small tumbler, but you can use either.

Use fresh peach purée if you wish. Alternatively, take a peach, blanch it in hot water to remove the skin, pit it, then blend it with a little dash of prosecco. Fill one third of your glass with the peach purée and top *carefully* with prosecco as it will fizz up manically. Stir as you are pouring, to fill the glass.

The junior version of this is a Virgin Bellini, where you replace the prosecco with club soda. Often a dash of sugar helps.

## caipirinha

This is a traditional Brazilian drink made with the local spirit, cachaça, and the local citrus fruit, limon (little green limes with seeds). There are many different ways of making this drink—this version is the way Dick was taught to make it by an eccentric Brazilian gentleman. To replicate the flavor of hard-to-find cachaça, use almost 2 shots (2 ounces) of light rum and a splash of tequila.

You will need to crush some ice first. You can do this by placing it in a bag, covering it with a kitchen towel and bashing it with a rolling pin, as you would if you were making a crumble base out of biscuits. Take a lime, chop the ends off it and cut it into about 16 small pieces. Put in a glass tumbler, coat with about 2 teaspoons of sugar syrup (see page 266) and crush the limes to release their oils into the sugar. People often use brown sugar or white sugar instead of sugar syrup in the belief that this accelerates the releasing of the oils, so experiment. You can use the end of a rolling pin to do this, but be careful, as you are using pressure in a glass. Fill the glass with crushed ice and add 2 ounces of cachaça. Stir and drink!

## daiquiri natural

This drink must be made to the exact recipe measurements, as you are playing with the sourness of lime set against the sweetness of rum, and if you don't get it exact the resulting imbalance in the flavor will be very obvious. The ratio is 8 parts rum to 2 parts lime and will only work with the correct rum, Havana Club, although other rums will have to do if you cannot find it.

For one drink, pour 2 ounces of Havana Club rum, 2½ teaspoons of freshly squeezed lime juice and 1 teaspoon of sugar syrup (see page 266) into a shaker. Add lightly cracked ice cubes and shake thoroughly until the shaker becomes frosted, then strain through a mesh, such as a tea strainer, into a prechilled cocktail glass.

## mojito

This is Dick's favorite summer drink for when he's relaxing in his hammock. You can make this with vodka or tequila, or even cachaça if you want, but for the true Cuban feel you do need Cuban rum. Place 3–5 small mint leaves in a glass. Coat with 2–3 teaspoons of sugar syrup (see page 266) and crush to release the mint oil. Add the juice of 1 fresh lime and 2 ounces of Havana Club rum. Fill the glass with crushed or cracked ice. You can add a little club soda if you wish. Stir thoroughly before drinking.

# watermelon vodka

This is a really funny thing that I saw an American friend of mine make. Great for a barbie or party. Wish I'd known about this when I was going to school parties—I could have walked in with my watermelon and got all my mates completely sloshed! Needs to be started three days—even a week—before you plan to eat it.

1 large, ripe watermelon—give it a smell and
   a slap to check for ripeness
1 bottle of best vodka (or even champagne)

Simply cut a hole in the top of the melon, wide and deep enough to insert a funnel. Make sure the funnel fits quite tightly or the liquid will spill out. If this happens, cut a larger hole. Pour some of your chosen alcohol into the melon through the funnel, leave to sit for a day and pour in some more. The flesh will absorb the liquid, so pour in some more the next day—basically until it becomes saturated. When ready to serve, slice up into nice big pieces and get all your mates plastered on it!

## frothy malted milk balls

1 package of malted milk balls
1 cup cold milk

In a blender or food processor, whizz up the
malted milk balls to a powder and add the milk until frothy.

# smoothies

I love smoothies, because you can make them with anything you like. Here's a basic smoothie recipe which you can flavor with 2–3 handfuls of any chosen fruit. Or flavor it using one of the three fantastic combinations given below.

*for 2 people*
1 banana
2–3 large handfuls of your chosen fruit
approximately 2½ cups of ice
1 cup light cream

Place the banana and your chosen fruit into a blender and whizz for 30 seconds. Add the ice and cream. Place the lid back on tightly and pulse a couple of times on and off to break up the larger pieces of ice before whizzing up to a semi-slushy milk shake consistency.

    If you haven't got a blender, you can do as I have been known to do—place the ice into a clean kitchen towel and bash the hell out of it with a rolling pin before stirring in the mushed fruit and the cream. It's good, but not quite as good. The 3 smoothies below can be made by following this basic recipe, using the listed ingredients as your chosen fruit.

## blackberry and pineapple smoothie

2 handfuls of blackberries
1 handful of peeled and chopped fresh pineapple

## banana and honey smoothie

1 more banana
2 tablespoons honey
2 heaped tablespoons peanut butter (if you're very sad)

## raspberry and strawberry smoothie

1 handful of raspberries
2 handfuls of strawberries

stocks, sauces,
bits, bobs, this,
that and the other

# chicken stock

*for 7 pints of stock*
4$\frac{1}{2}$lb raw chicken carcasses, chopped
$\frac{1}{2}$ a head of garlic, broken up but unpeeled
6 handfuls of fragrant root vegetables (celery, onions, carrots), chopped
3 bay leaves
3 handfuls of mixed fresh herbs (rosemary, parsley, thyme)
5 whole black peppercorns
8$\frac{3}{4}$ pints cold water

Chuck all the ingredients into a large, deep pan and bring to the boil. Turn the heat down and simmer for 1–3 hours, skimming as necessary. Pass through a sieve, and once cool you can keep it in the fridge for 4 days or the freezer for up to 3 months.

# fish stock

*for 5 pints of stock*
6 handfuls of fragrant root vegetables (celery, fennel, onion), chopped
$\frac{1}{2}$ a head of garlic, broken up and sliced thinly
2 dried red chillies
4$\frac{1}{2}$lb fish bones, chopped and washed thoroughly
2 tablespoons olive oil
1 cup plus 2 tablespoons dry white wine
6 pints cold water
6 sprigs of fresh parsley
1 sprig of fresh thyme

In a large, deep pan, slowly fry the vegetables, garlic, chillies and fish bones in olive oil until the vegetables are tender. Add the white wine and cook for another 2 or 3 minutes. Add the water and bring to the boil. Simmer for 20 minutes only, adding all the fresh herbs, and skim regularly. Pass through a sieve and allow to cool. Fish stock can be boiled and reduced to intensify its flavor. It can be stored in the fridge for about 2–3 days, or you can freeze it for 1–2 months. A sign of a good stock is when it's tasty, clear and, when cold, sets like jelly.

## vegetable stock

Half-fill your largest deep pan with roughly chopped fragrant vegetables such as celery, fennel, carrots, onions and leeks, and add plum tomatoes and garlic, and herbs and spices such as thyme, rosemary, bay, parsley and chilli. If you have any dried mushrooms add them too, as they give an amazing flavor. Cover with cold water, bring to the boil, and then simmer for 1–2 hours with a lid on the pan. Vegetable stock will keep in the fridge for a week and in the freezer for 2–3 months.

## garlic aïoli

*serves 8*
1 clove of garlic, peeled
1 teaspoon salt
1 large egg yolk
1 teaspoon Dijon mustard
approximately 1 cup extra-virgin olive oil
approximately 1 cup olive oil
lemon juice, to taste
salt and freshly ground black pepper

Smash up or finely chop the garlic and mix with the salt. Whisk the egg yolk and mustard together in a bowl, then slowly start to add the olive oil bit by bit—using two different types will give the aïoli a flavor which isn't too strong or too peppery. Once you've blended in a quarter of the olive oil, start to add the rest in larger amounts. Then add the garlic and lemon juice, along with any optional extra flavors such as basil, fennel tops or dill. Season to taste, adding a little extra lemon juice to taste.

stocks, sauces, bits, bobs, this, that and the other

# tomato salsa

A really fantastic salsa which is brilliant served with tuna or swordfish. You can remove the skin of the tomatoes if you wish—I quite like the skin left on for this one.

*serves 4–6*

2 good handfuls of really ripe plum
   tomatoes, seeded and finely chopped

1 good handful of small capers,
   soaked and drained

2 small shallots or 1/2 a red onion,
   finely chopped

1/2 a clove of garlic, finely chopped

1 good handful of flat-leaf parsley,
   finely chopped

a couple of swigs of balsamic vinegar,
   to taste

6–8 glugs of olive oil

dried chilli flakes, to taste

4 anchovy fillets, finely chopped

1/2 a cucumber, peeled, seeded and
   finely diced

salt and freshly ground black pepper, to taste

Mix all the ingredients together, season to taste, and you have a brilliant salsa.

# salsa verde

The secret of a good salsa verde is to chop all the ingredients very fine and to use it the same day, as it doesn't tend to keep for long, even in the fridge. A fantastic accompaniment to any grilled meat or fish. Particularly good with the sea bass recipe on page 156.

*serves 8*

2 cloves of garlic, peeled

1 small handful of capers

1 small handful of pickled gherkins
   (the ones in sweet vinegar)

6 anchovy fillets

2 large handfuls of flat-leaf parsley,
   leaves picked from stems

1 bunch of fresh basil, leaves picked

1 handful of fresh mint, leaves picked

1 tablespoon Dijon mustard

3 tablespoons red wine vinegar

approximately 1/2 cup of your best olive
   oil

sea salt and freshly ground black pepper

Finely chop the first seven ingredients and put them into a bowl. Add the mustard and red wine vinegar, then slowly stir in the olive oil. Balance the flavors with freshly ground black pepper and, if necessary, sea salt and a little more red wine vinegar.

## minted bread sauce

*serves 4*
3 handfuls of fresh mint
1 handful of chopped bread
extra-virgin olive oil
salt and freshly ground black pepper
2 teaspoons English mustard
red wine vinegar

Finely chop 3 parts mint to 1 part bread and stir in some olive oil until the mix has "loosened." Then balance the flavors by carefully seasoning, adding the mustard and splashing in some vinegar to taste. The flavor improves with time.

## creamed horseradish

One of the most amazing sauces, this can turn round a simple piece of grilled or roasted beef or a roasted beet or carrot. Using the prepared stuff that comes in jars in this recipe can be delicious, but the fresh stuff is a million miles superior. If using fresh horseradish, which can be obtained from bigger supermarkets, peel and grate it.

Whether using prepared or fresh horseradish, put it in a bowl, adding crème frâiche to thin the sauce and mellow the flavor to your taste—in my case, hot. Season carefully with sea salt and freshly ground black pepper and a good splash of white wine vinegar.

# index

index

index

## thanks,
## nice one, shout going out,
## cheers, respect, much love

—      I'd like to thank a handful of very special people, because without their help, commitment and enthusiasm, this book wouldn't be the book it is today. Thank you very very much. My missus — sorry, the lovely Jules — for continuing to give me slap and tickle when need be. David Loftus, for being the most patient and nicest bloke and the best photographer in the world, and for letting me be godfather to his and Debs's daughter. My best man, Ben, for his friendship, support and indispensable help. Handsome Peter "Girth" Begg and the River Café posse. Mum and Dad for being "mum and dad." My sis, Anna, and new bro Paul for ideas. The biggest thanks in the world to Lindsey Jordan, for being my sidekick, keeping me in order, giving me loads of support and threatening me with violence when need be. You're the best food editor in town, babe. Tom Weldon, for letting me do what he promised. John Hamilton, for equaling my enthusiasm in the design and always thinking up new ideas for the whole look and vibe of the book, and being a dead cool Glaswegian geezer.

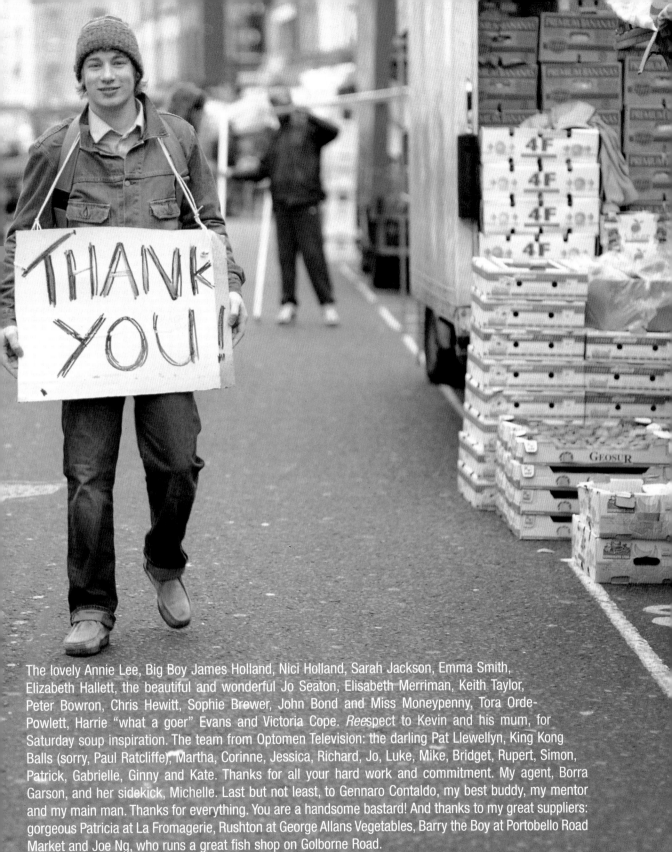

The lovely Annie Lee, Big Boy James Holland, Nici Holland, Sarah Jackson, Emma Smith, Elizabeth Hallett, the beautiful and wonderful Jo Seaton, Elisabeth Merriman, Keith Taylor, Peter Bowron, Chris Hewitt, Sophie Brewer, John Bond and Miss Moneypenny, Tora Orde-Powlett, Harrie "what a goer" Evans and Victoria Cope. *Ree*spect to Kevin and his mum, for Saturday soup inspiration. The team from Optomen Television: the darling Pat Llewellyn, King Kong Balls (sorry, Paul Ratcliffe), Martha, Corinne, Jessica, Richard, Jo, Luke, Mike, Bridget, Rupert, Simon, Patrick, Gabrielle, Ginny and Kate. Thanks for all your hard work and commitment. My agent, Borra Garson, and her sidekick, Michelle. Last but not least, to Gennaro Contaldo, my best buddy, my mentor and my main man. Thanks for everything. You are a handsome bastard! And thanks to my great suppliers: gorgeous Patricia at La Fromagerie, Rushton at George Allans Vegetables, Barry the Boy at Portobello Road Market and Joe Ng, who runs a great fish shop on Golborne Road.

the end